Coloring Book For Teenage Girls

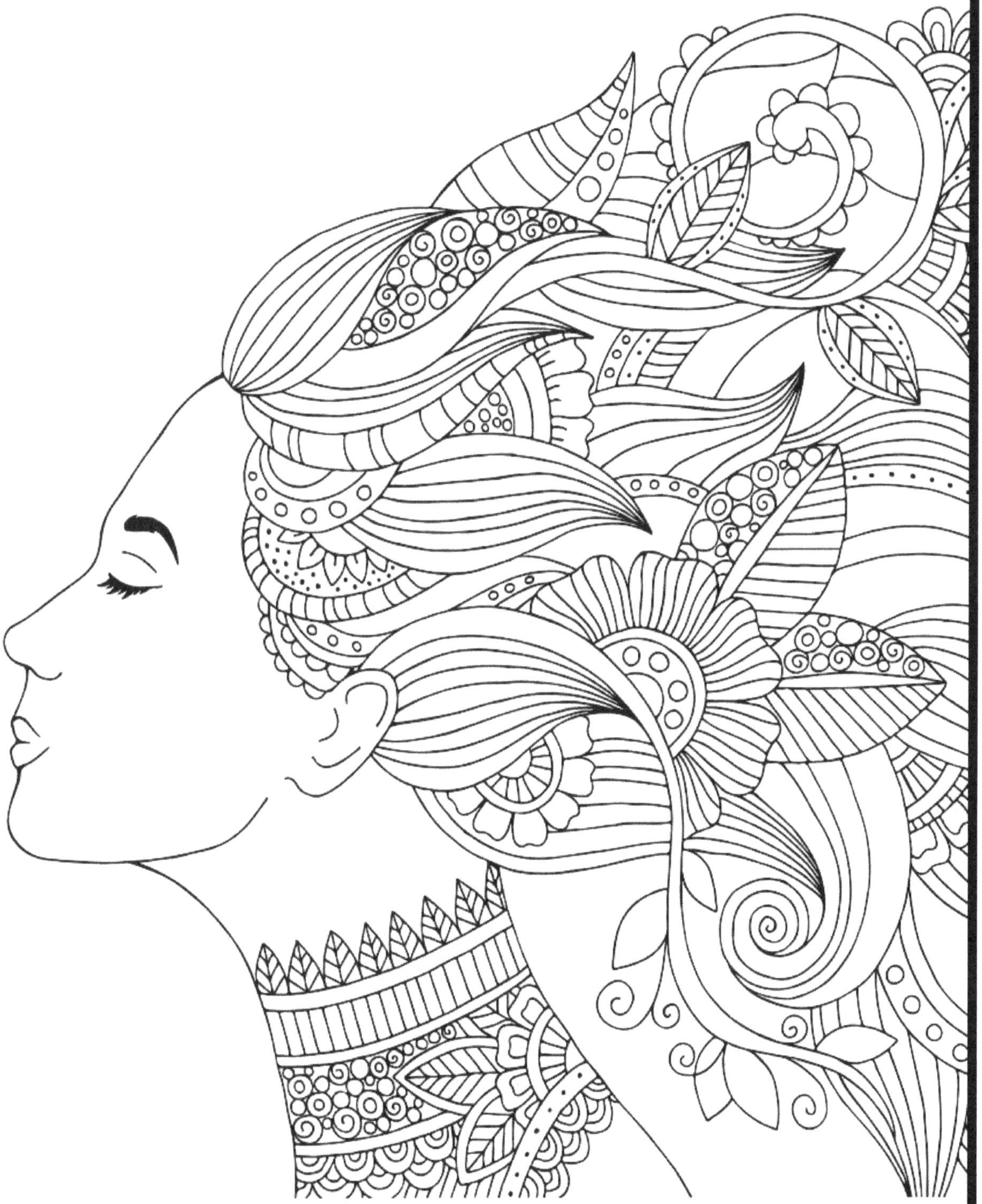

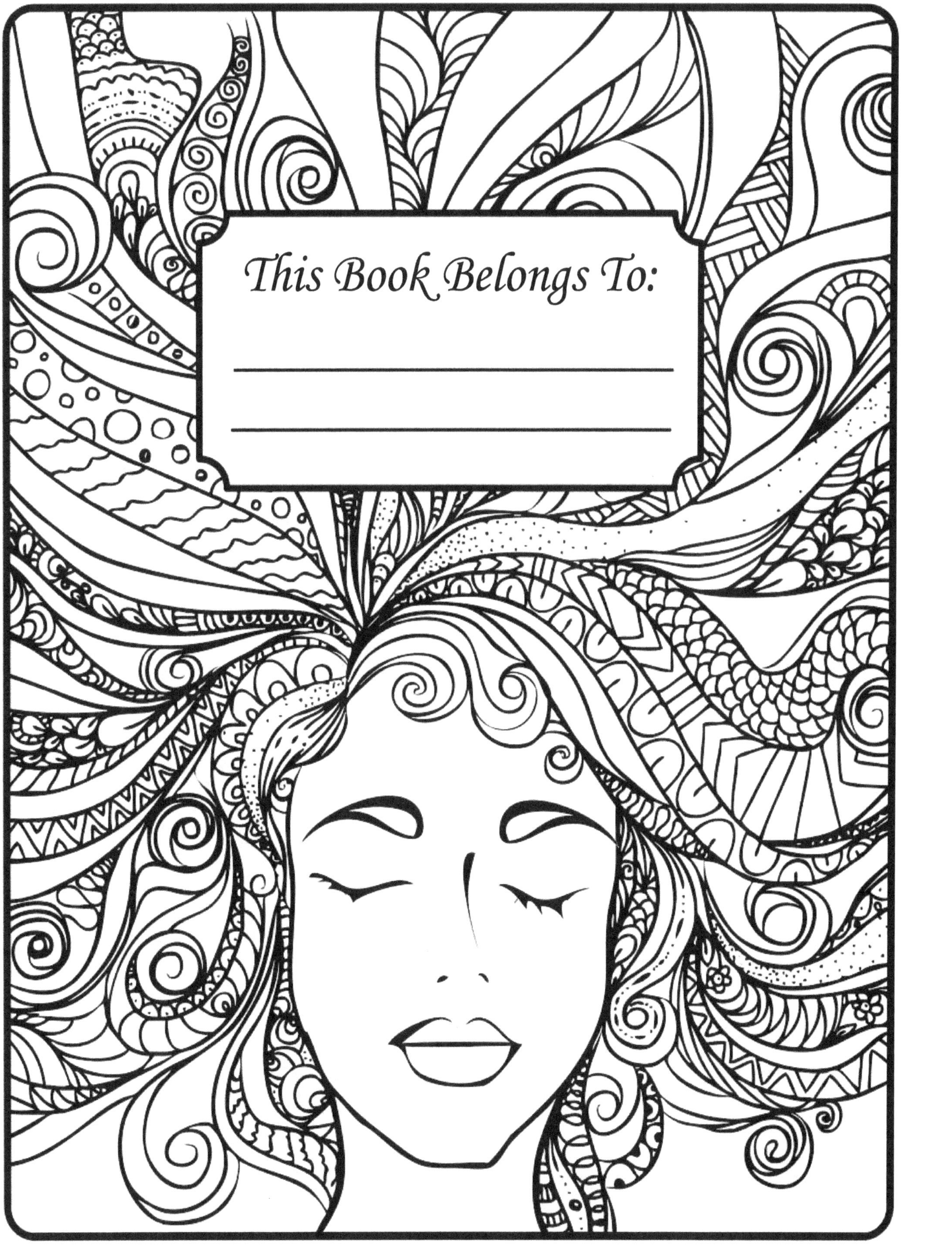
This Book Belongs To:

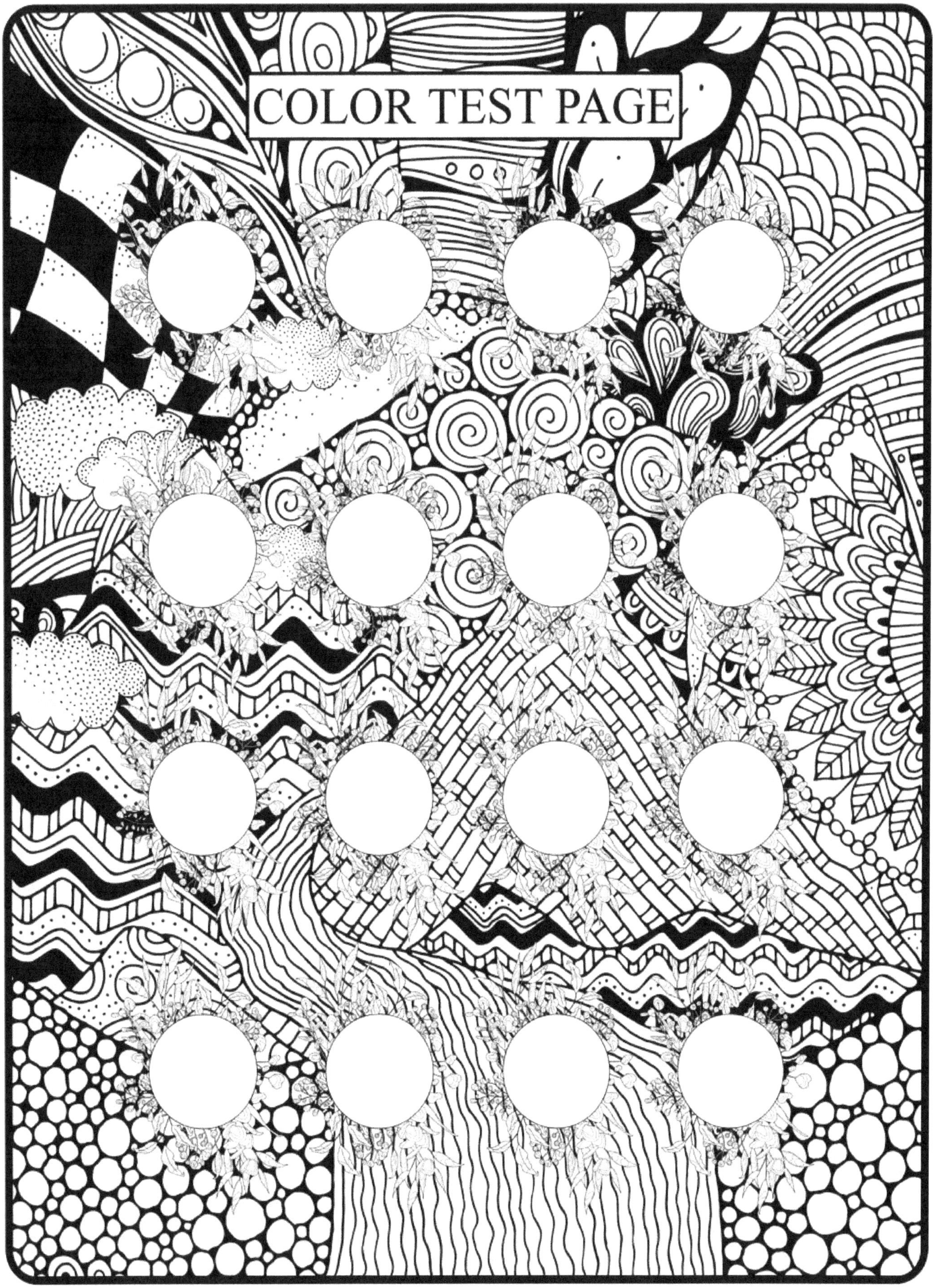
COLOR TEST PAGE

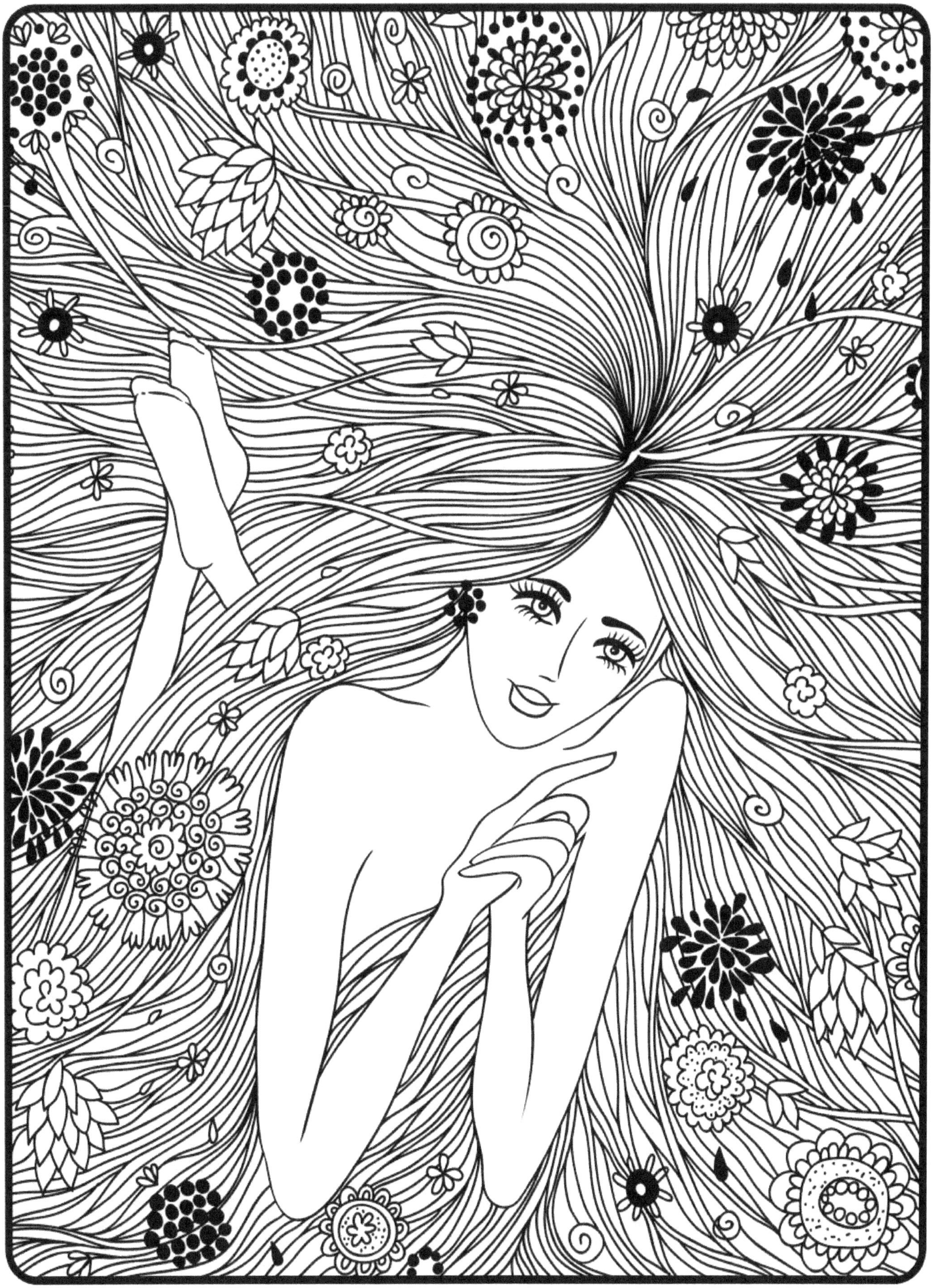

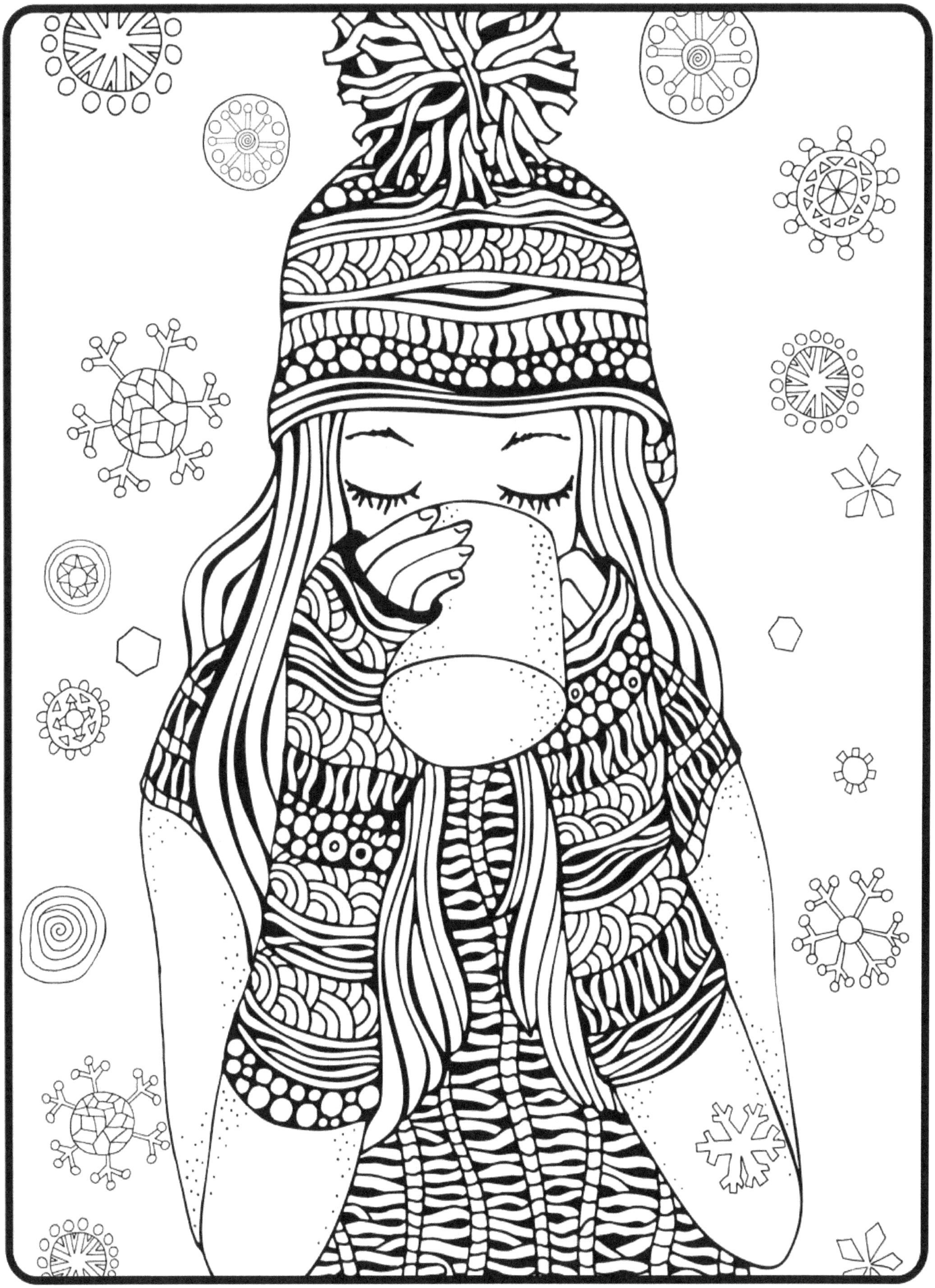

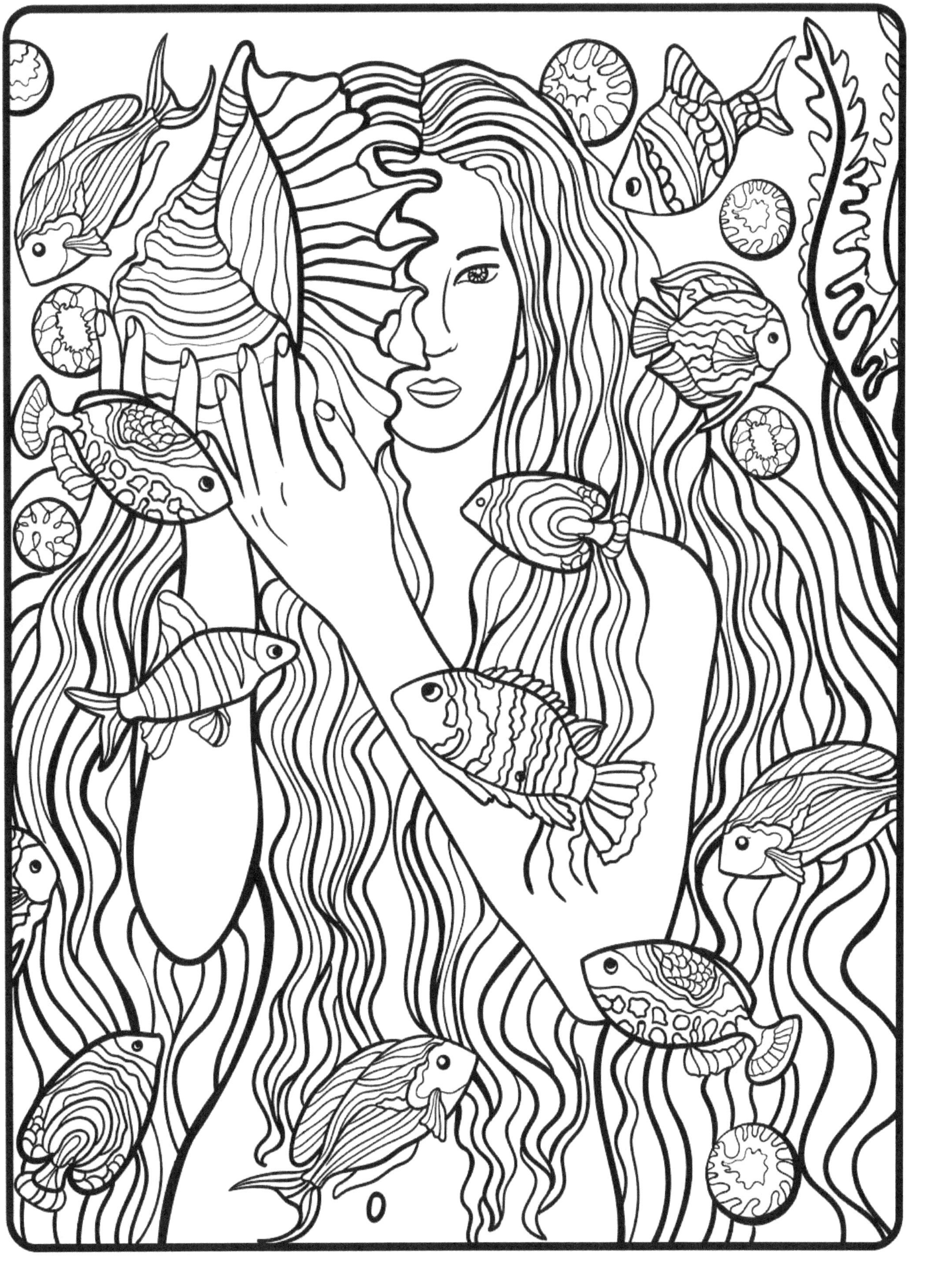

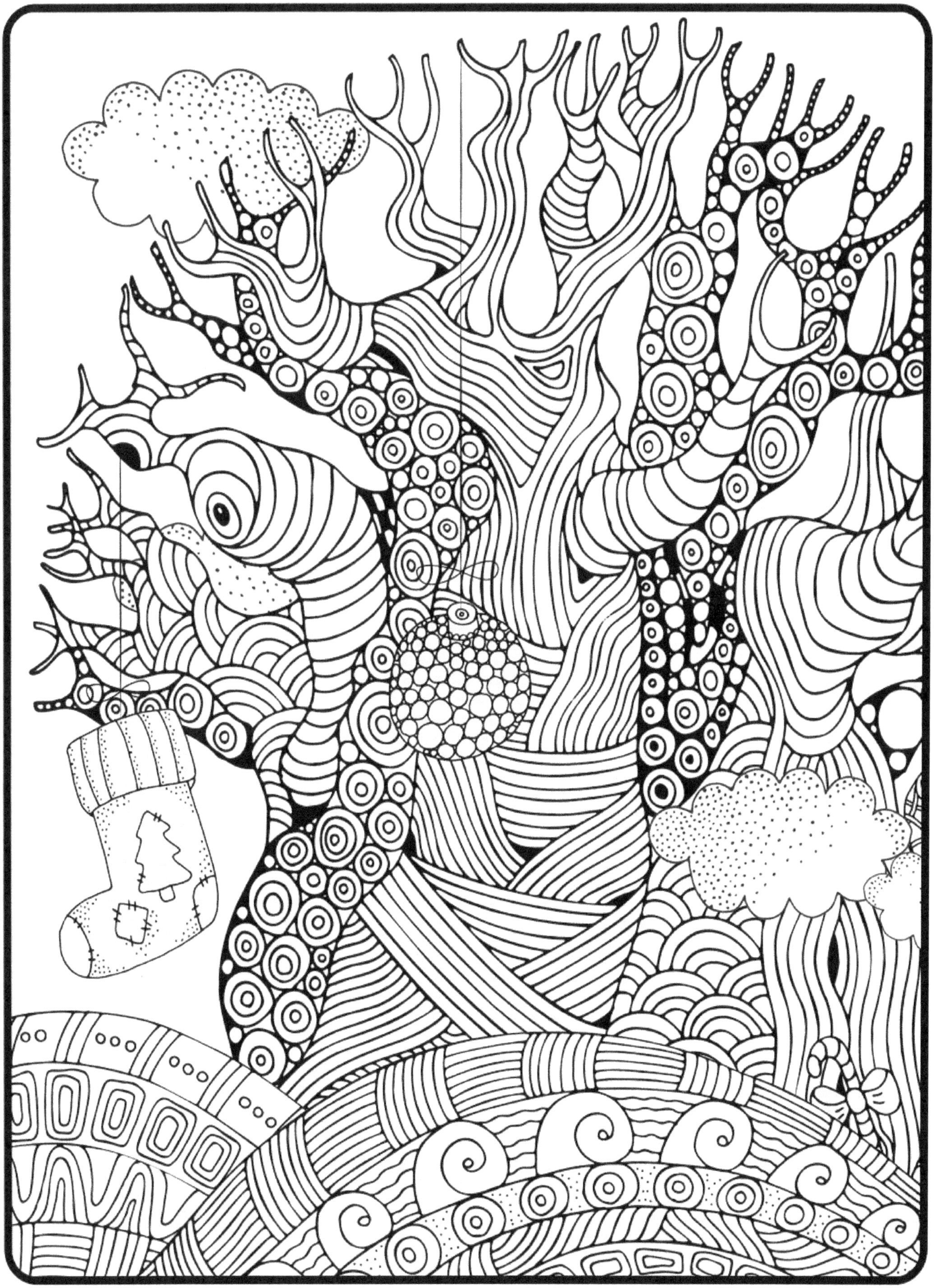

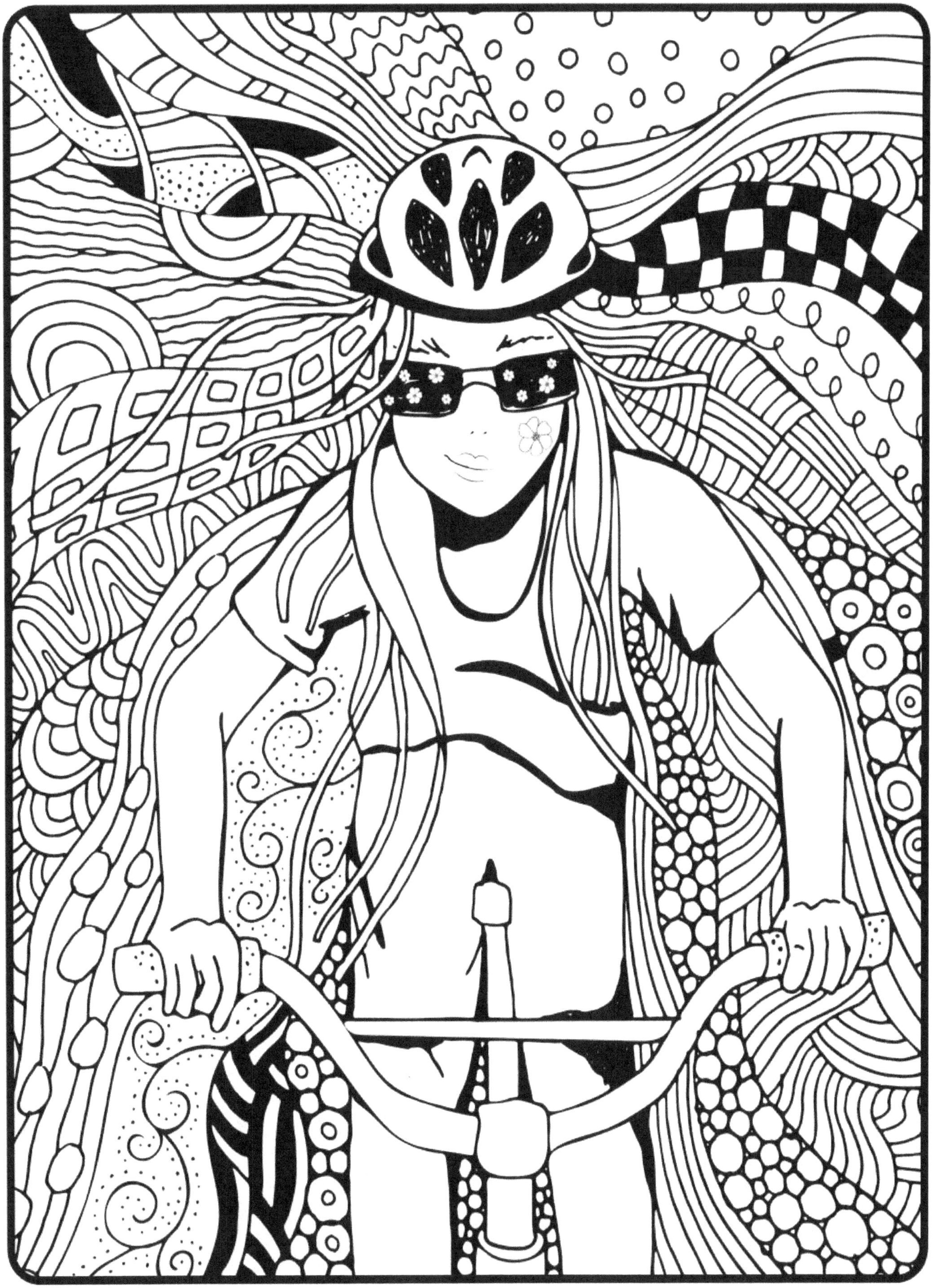

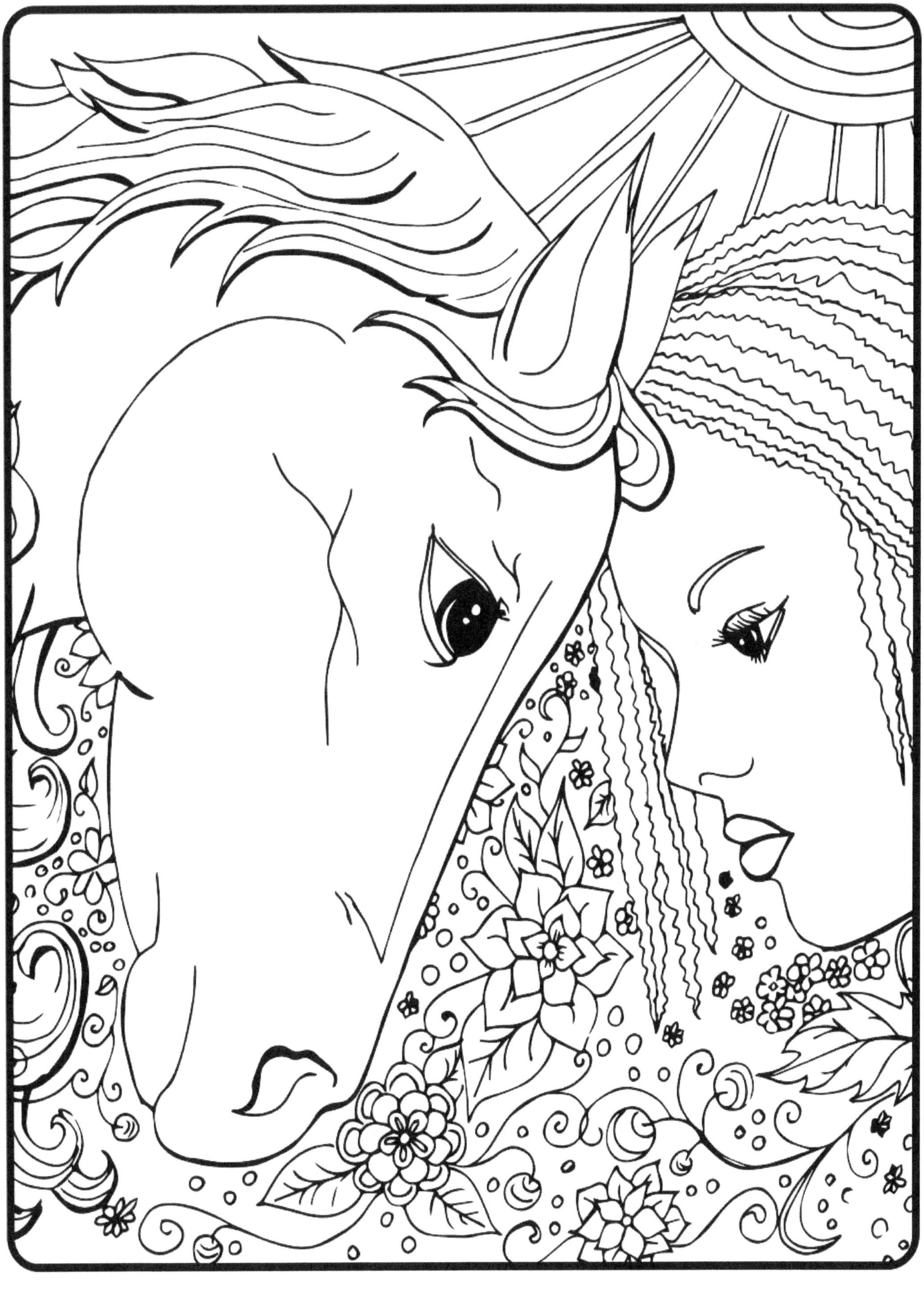

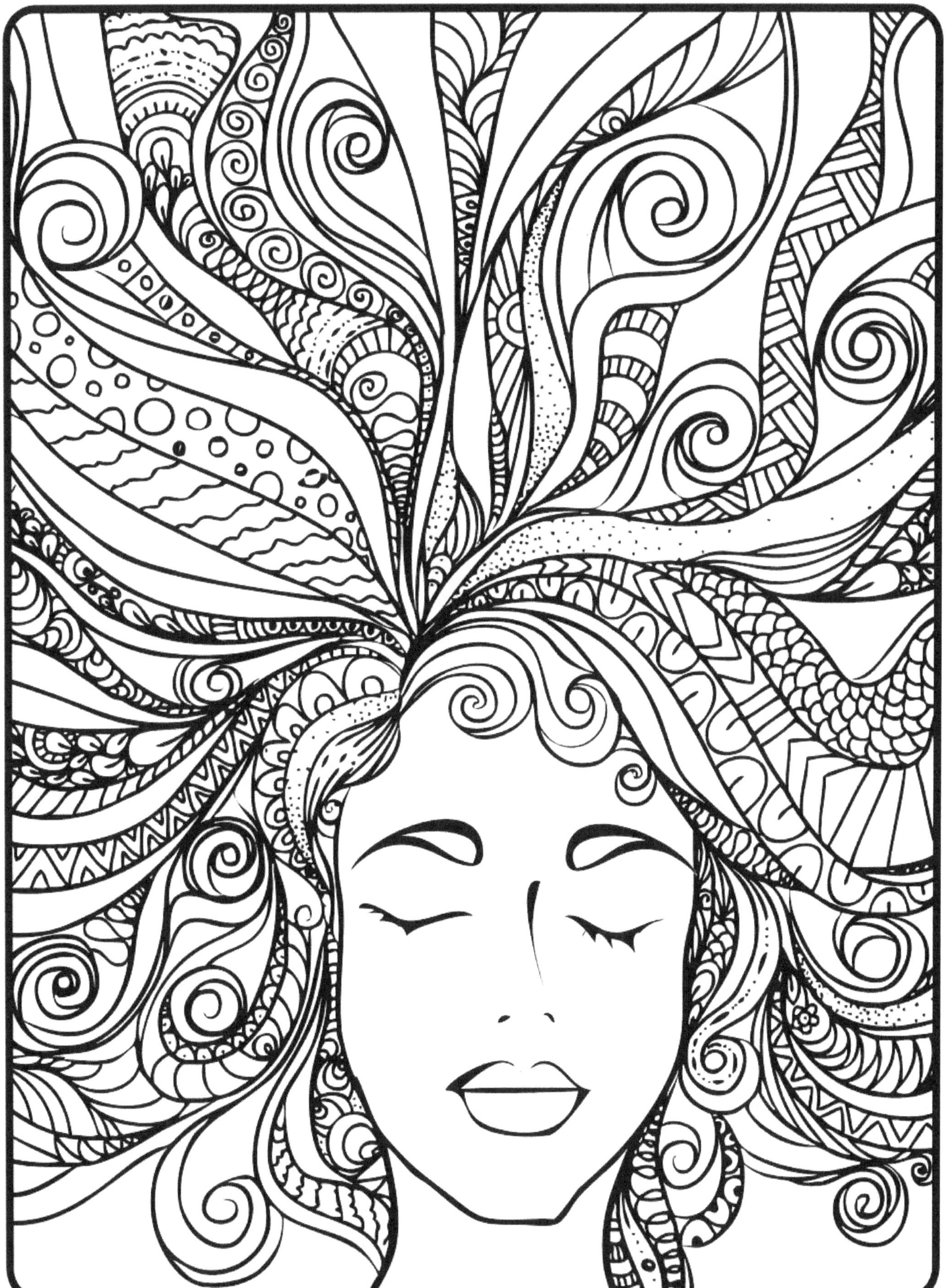

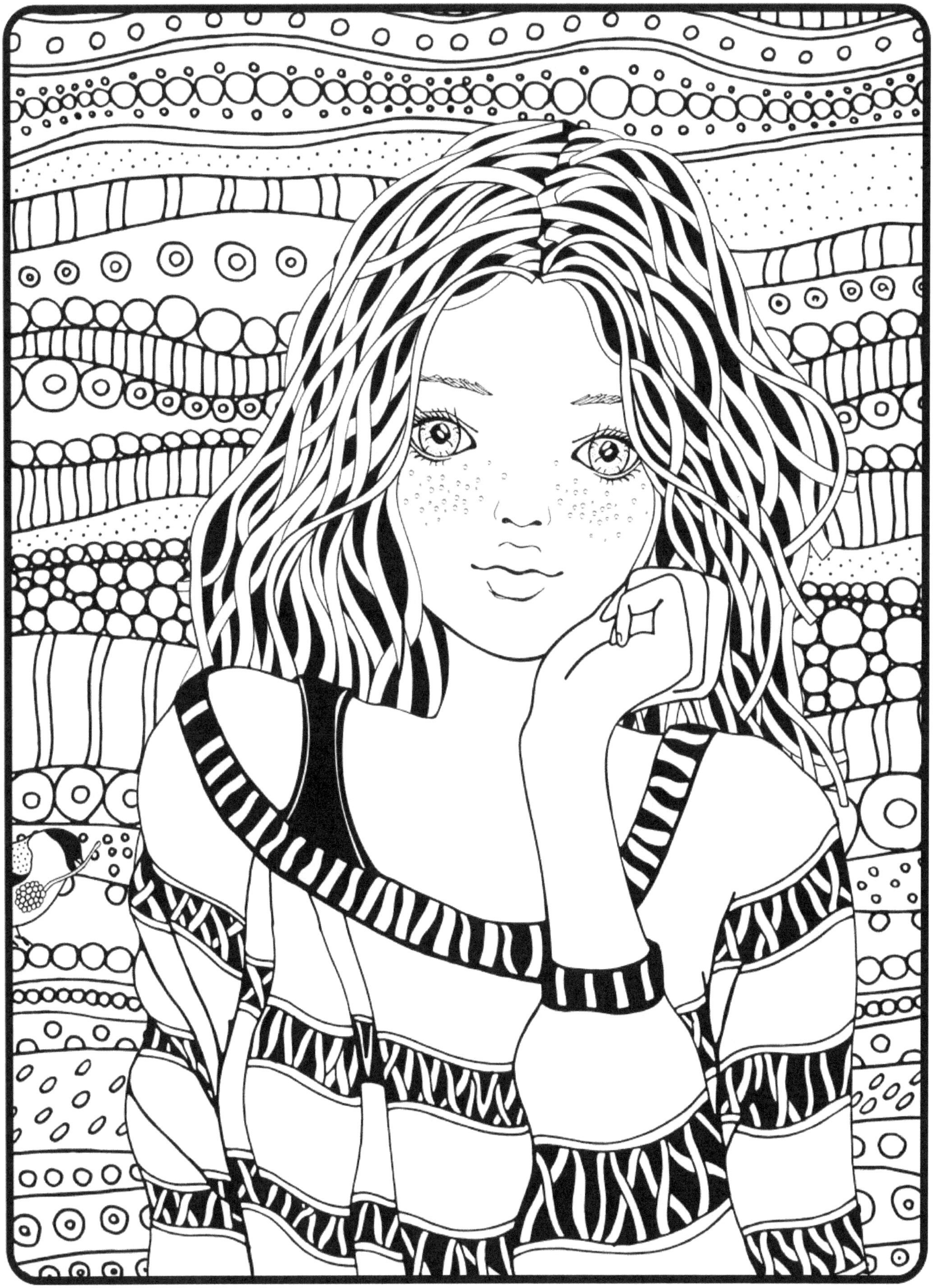

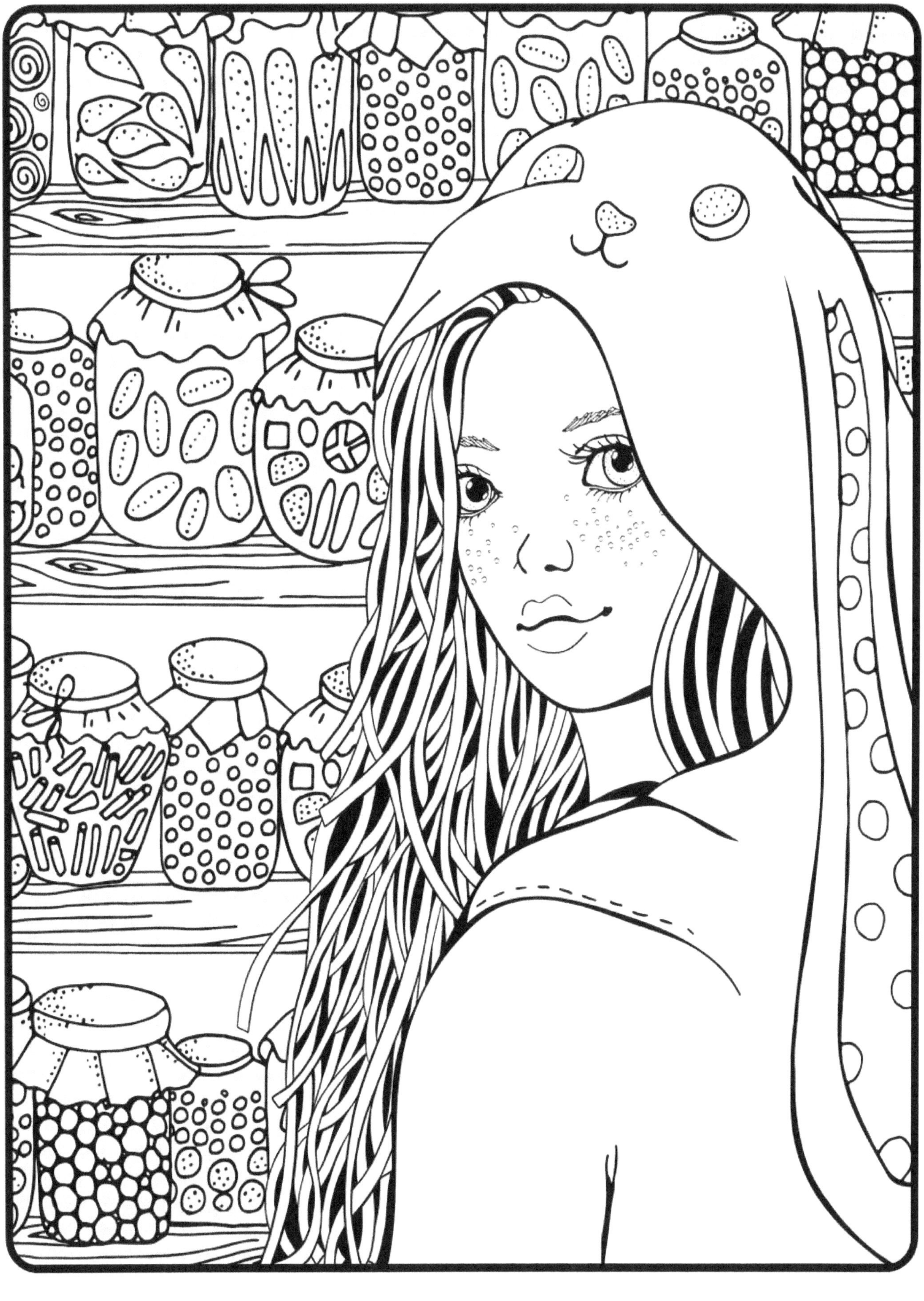

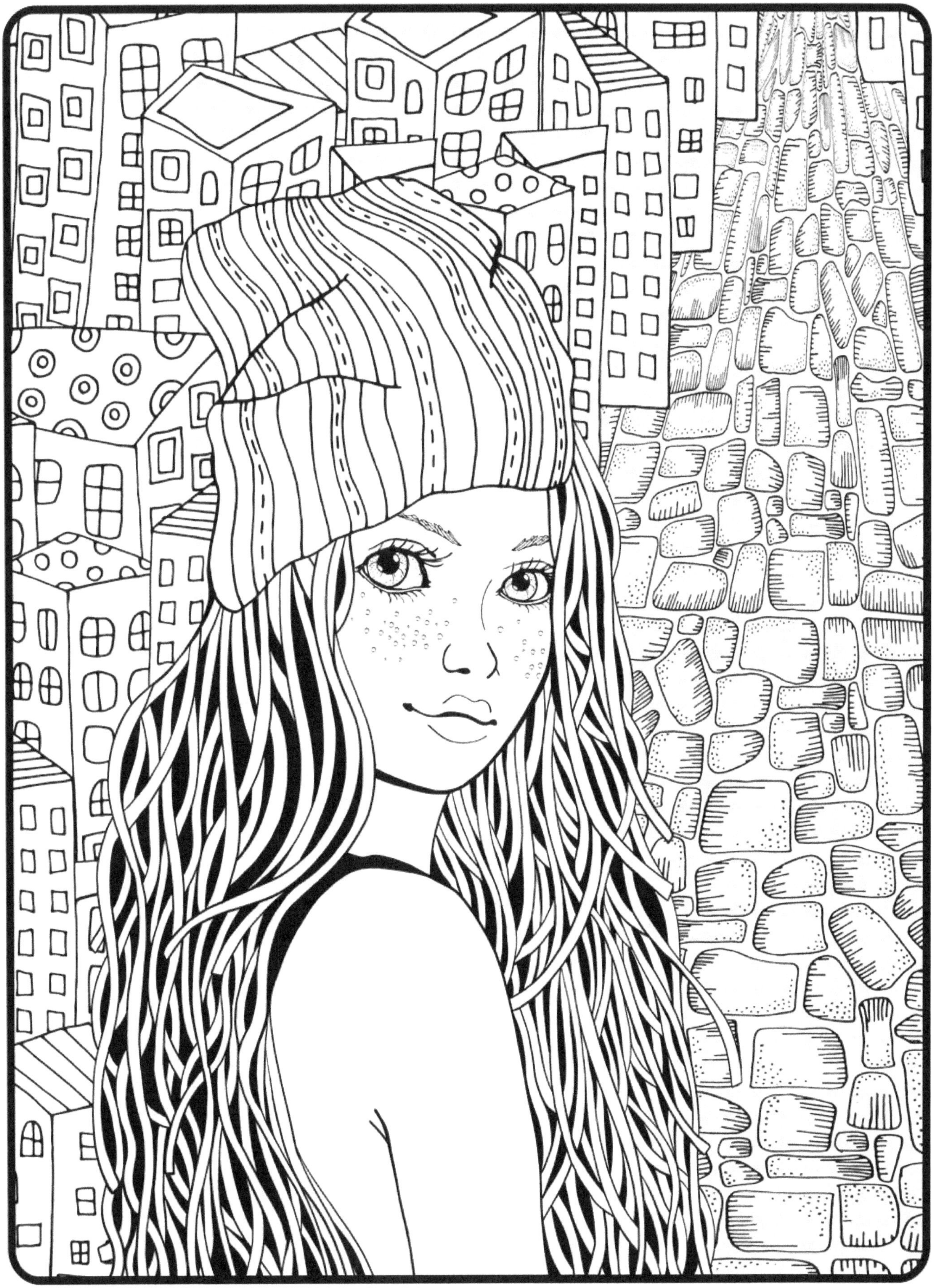

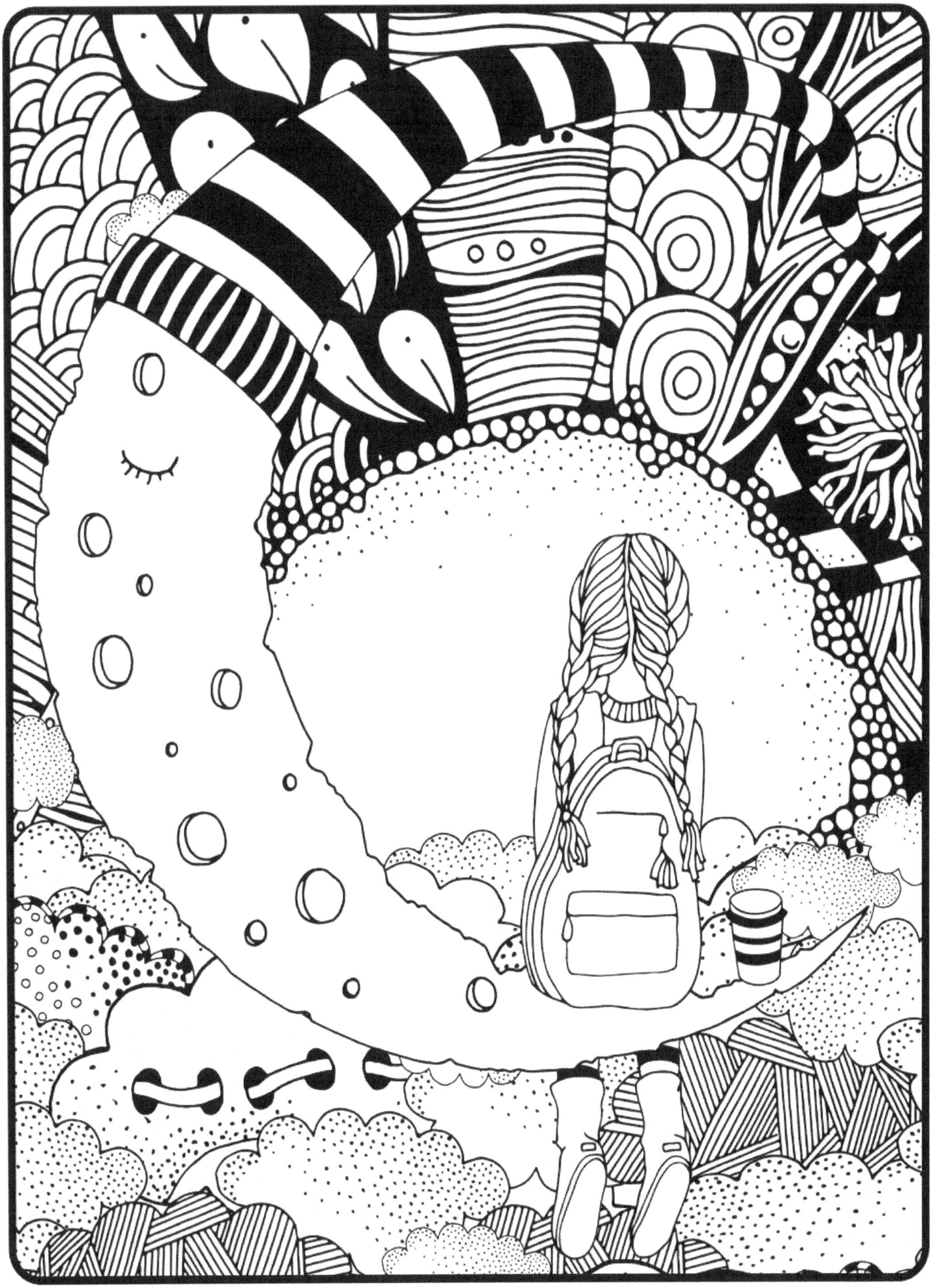

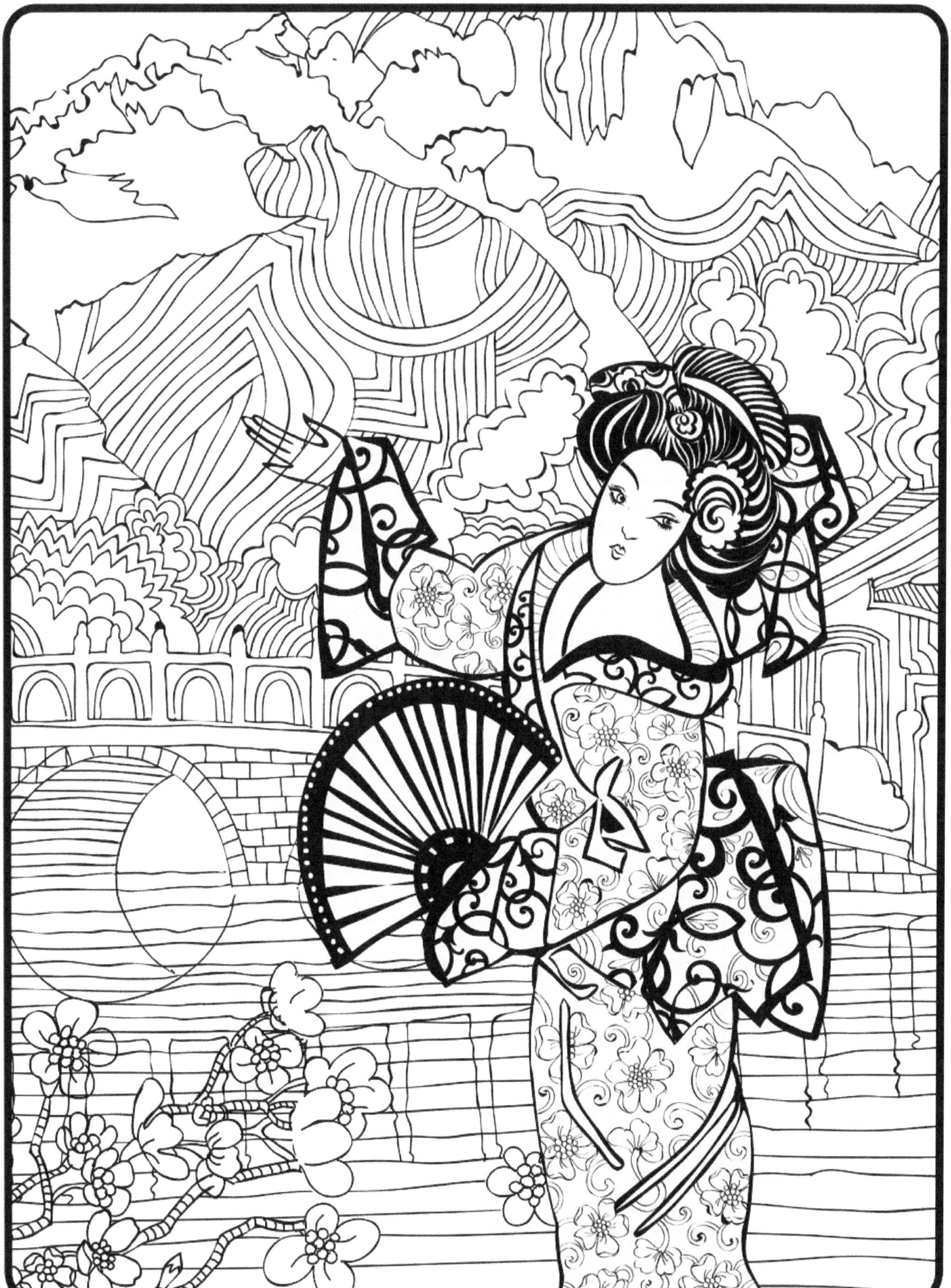

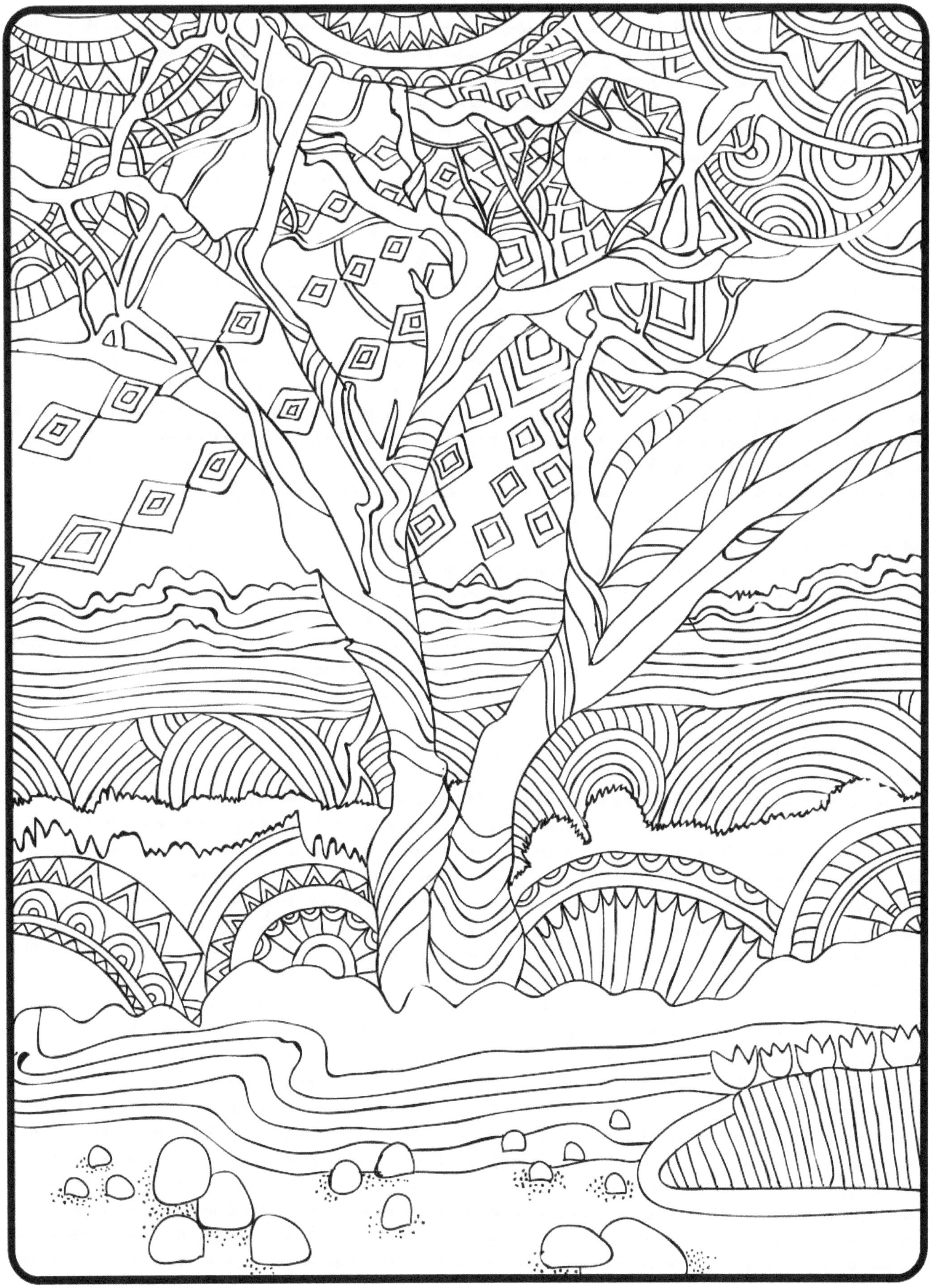

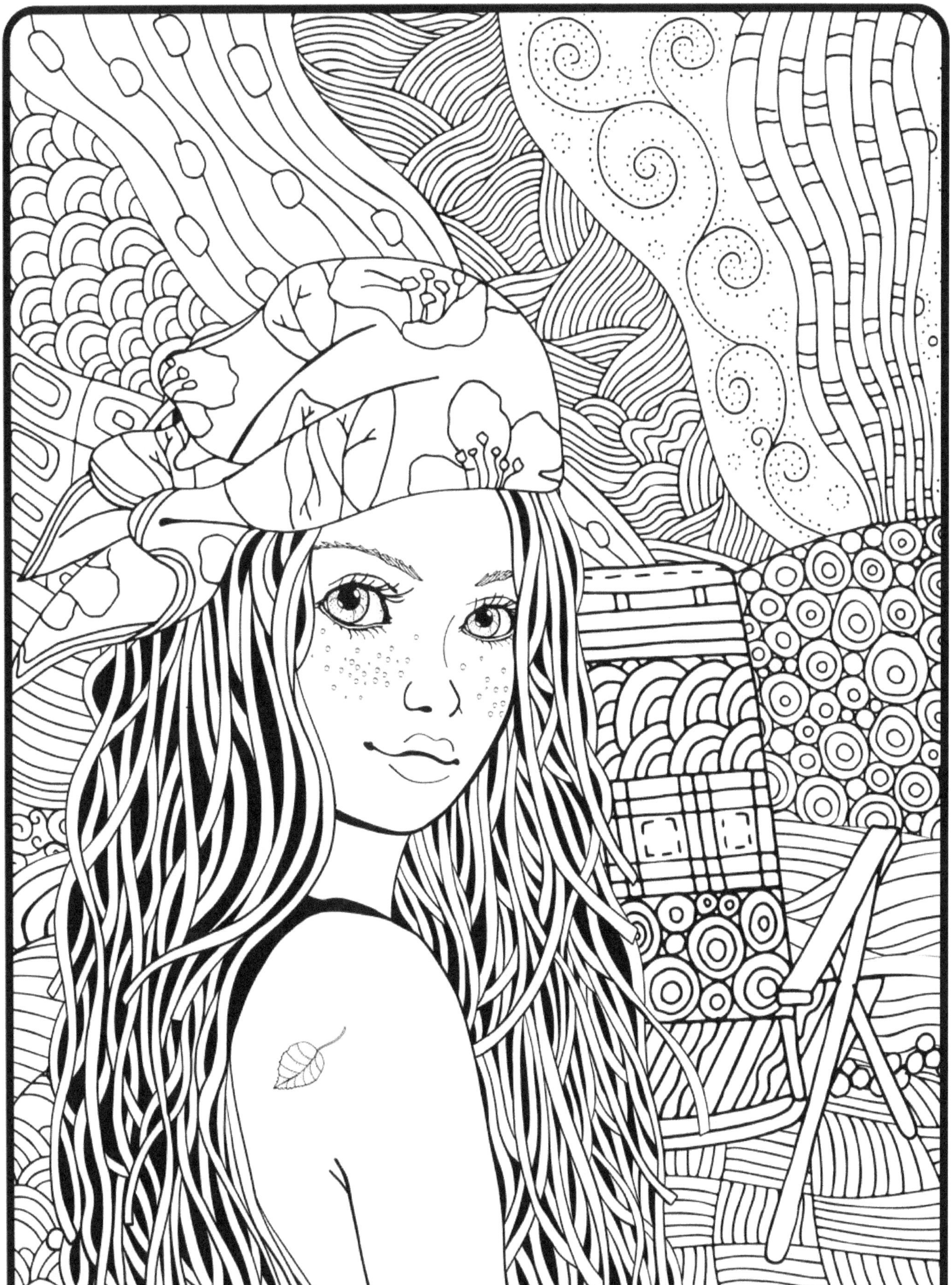

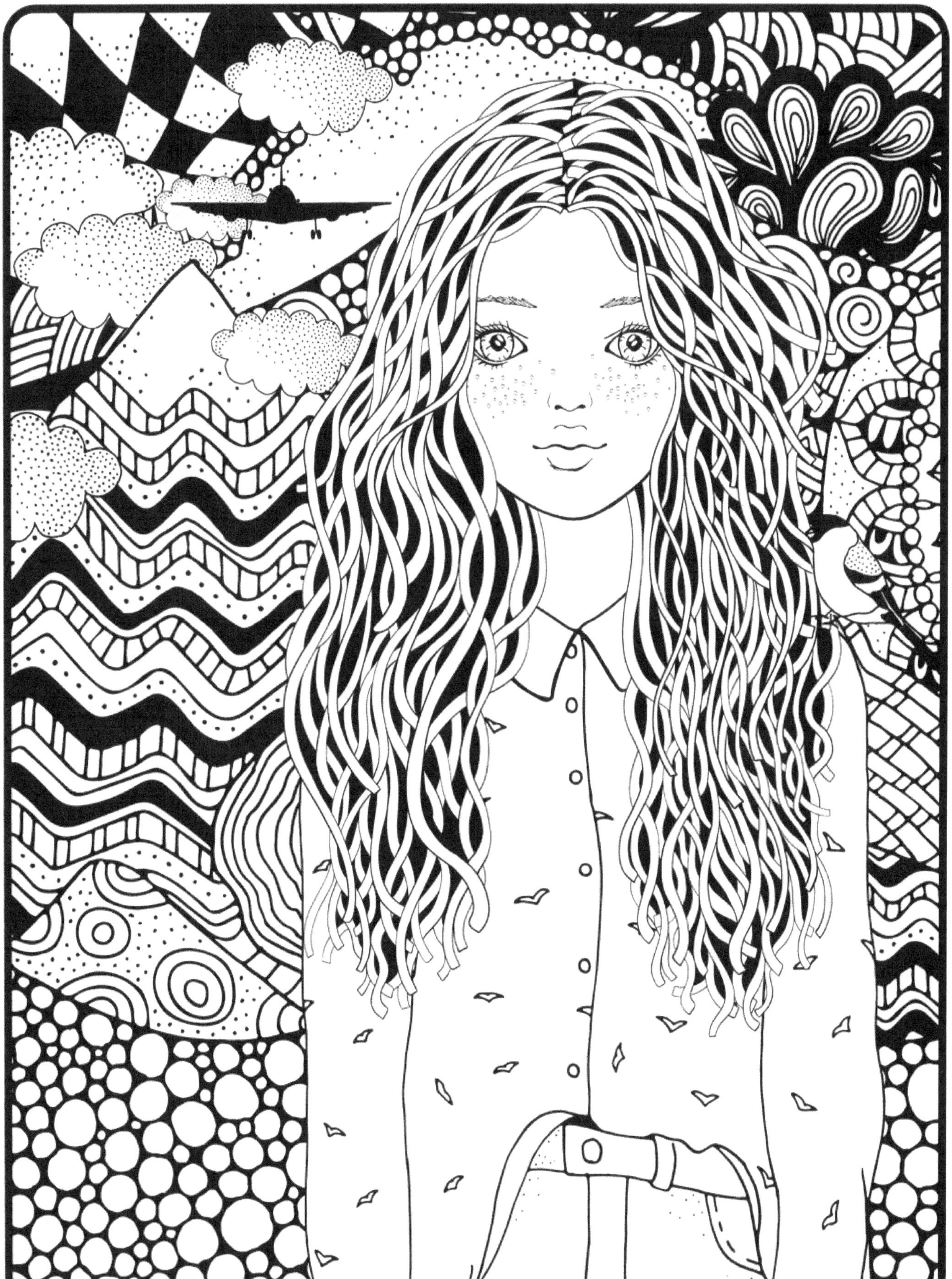

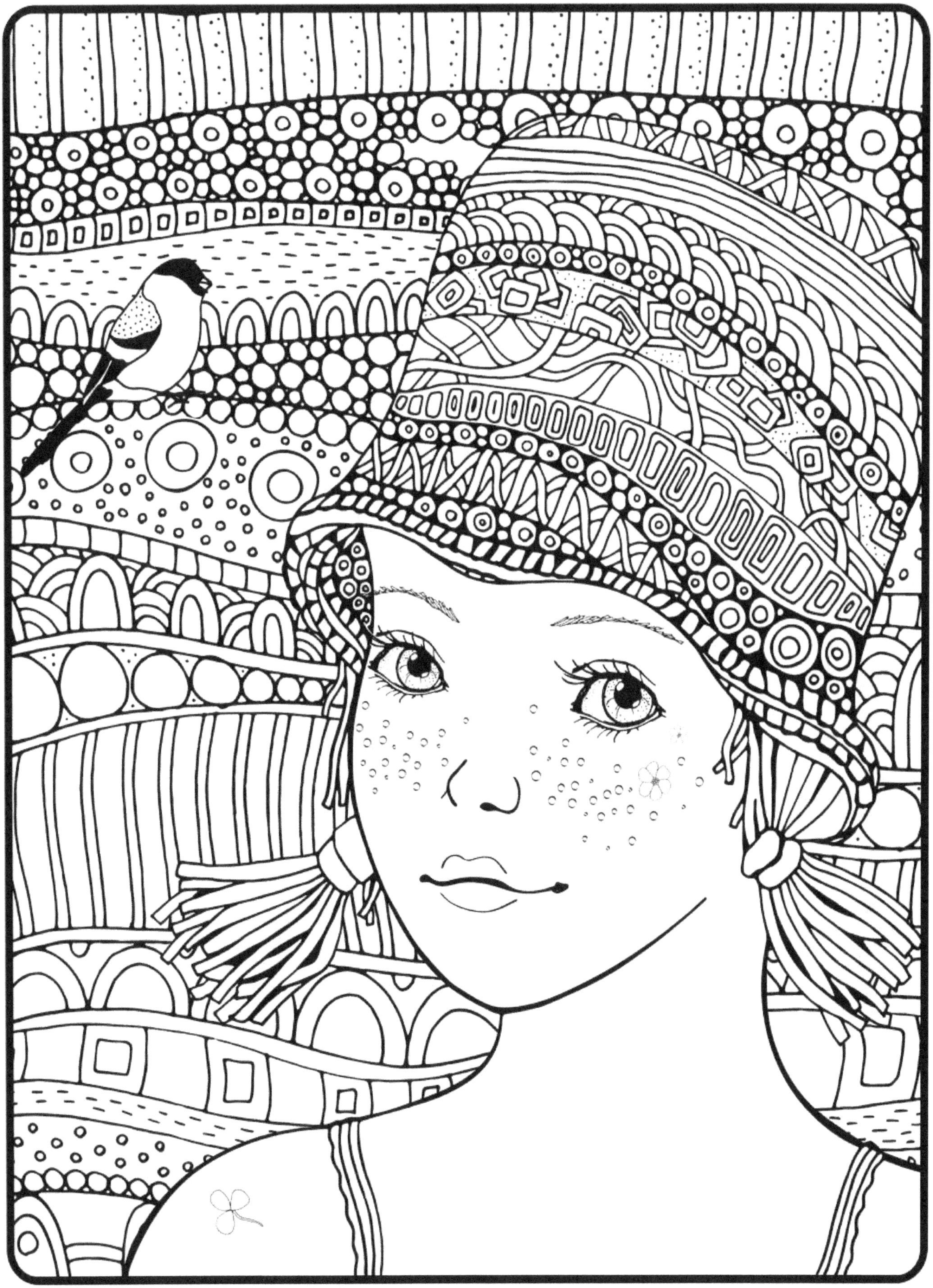

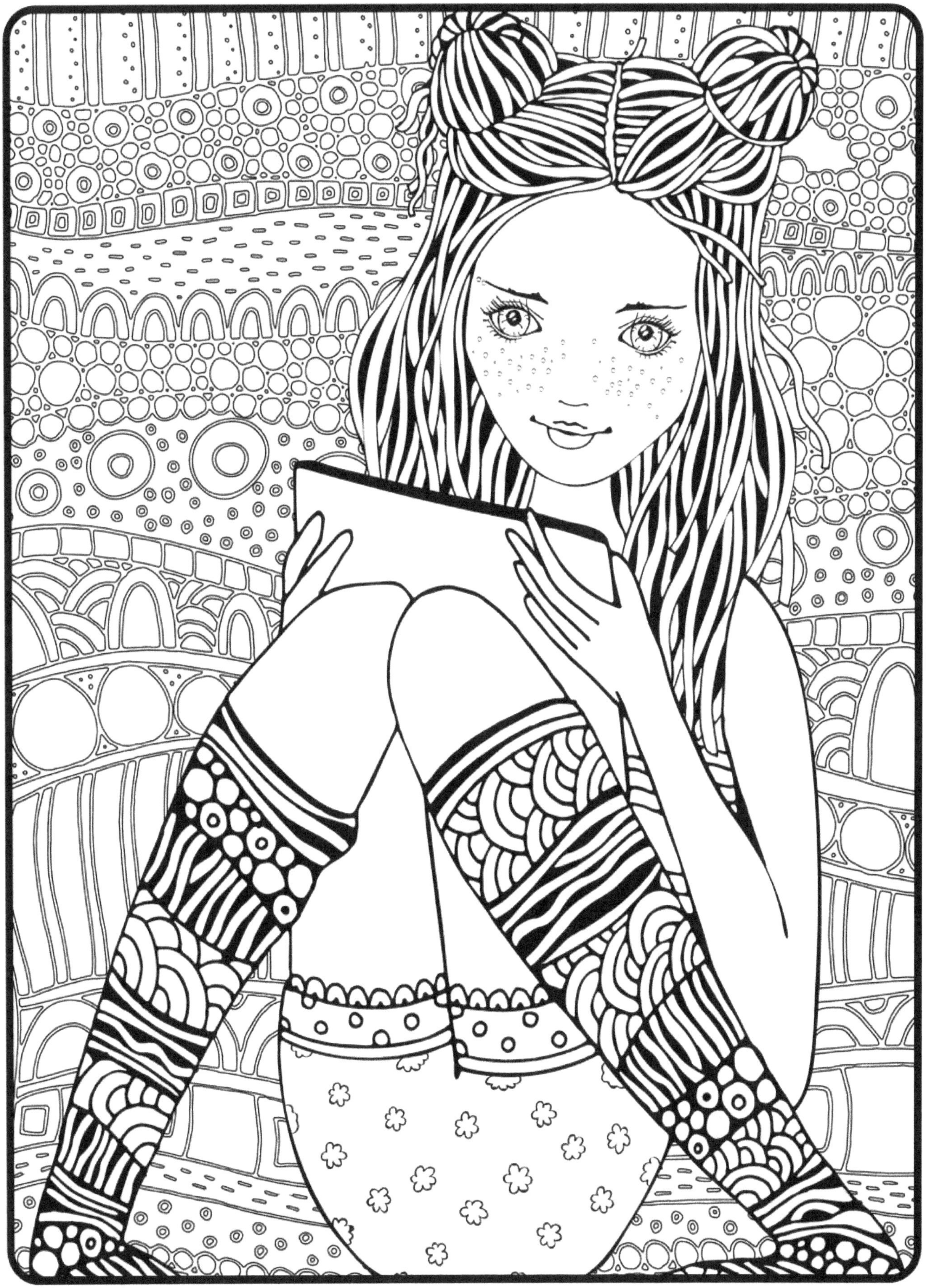

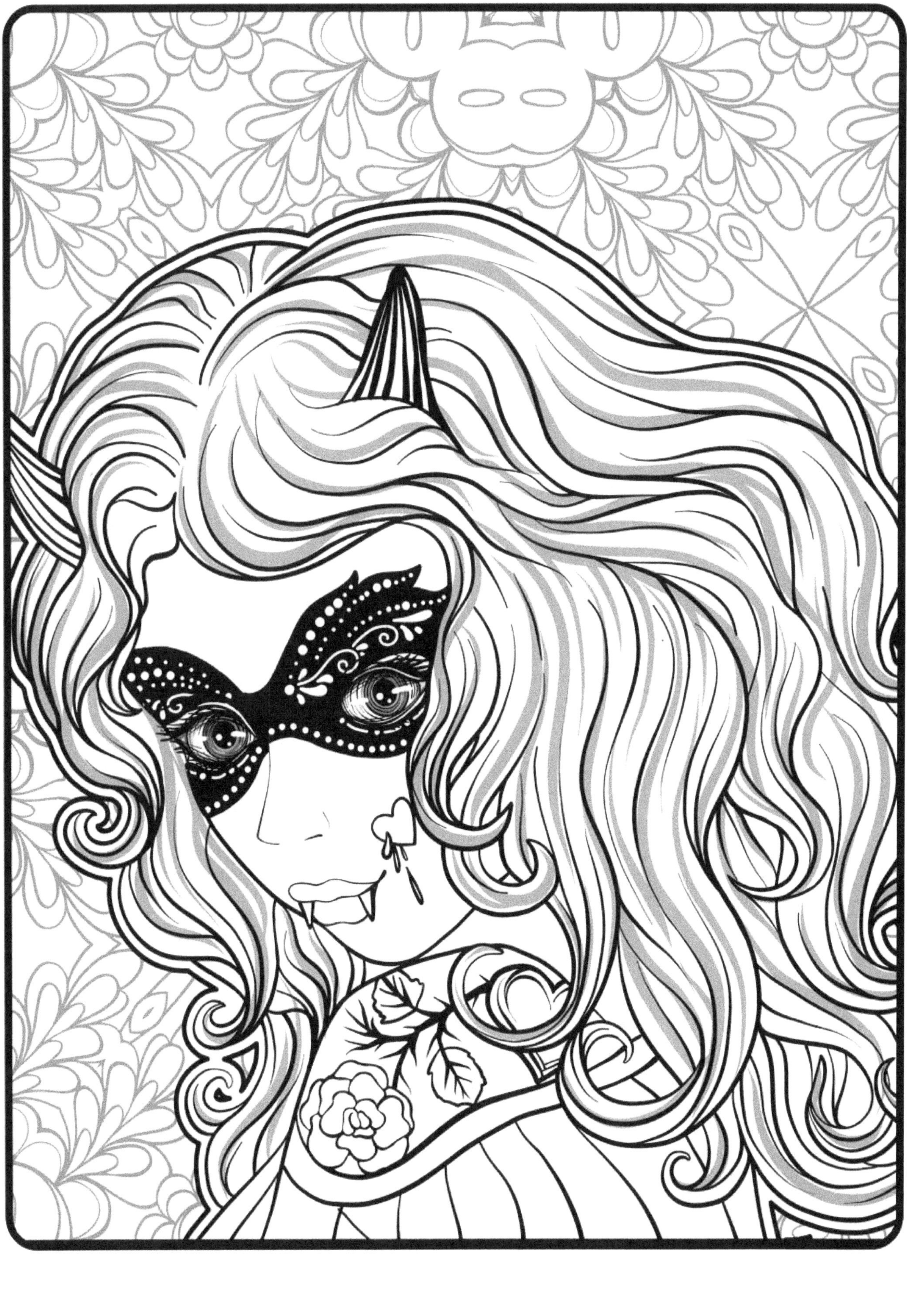

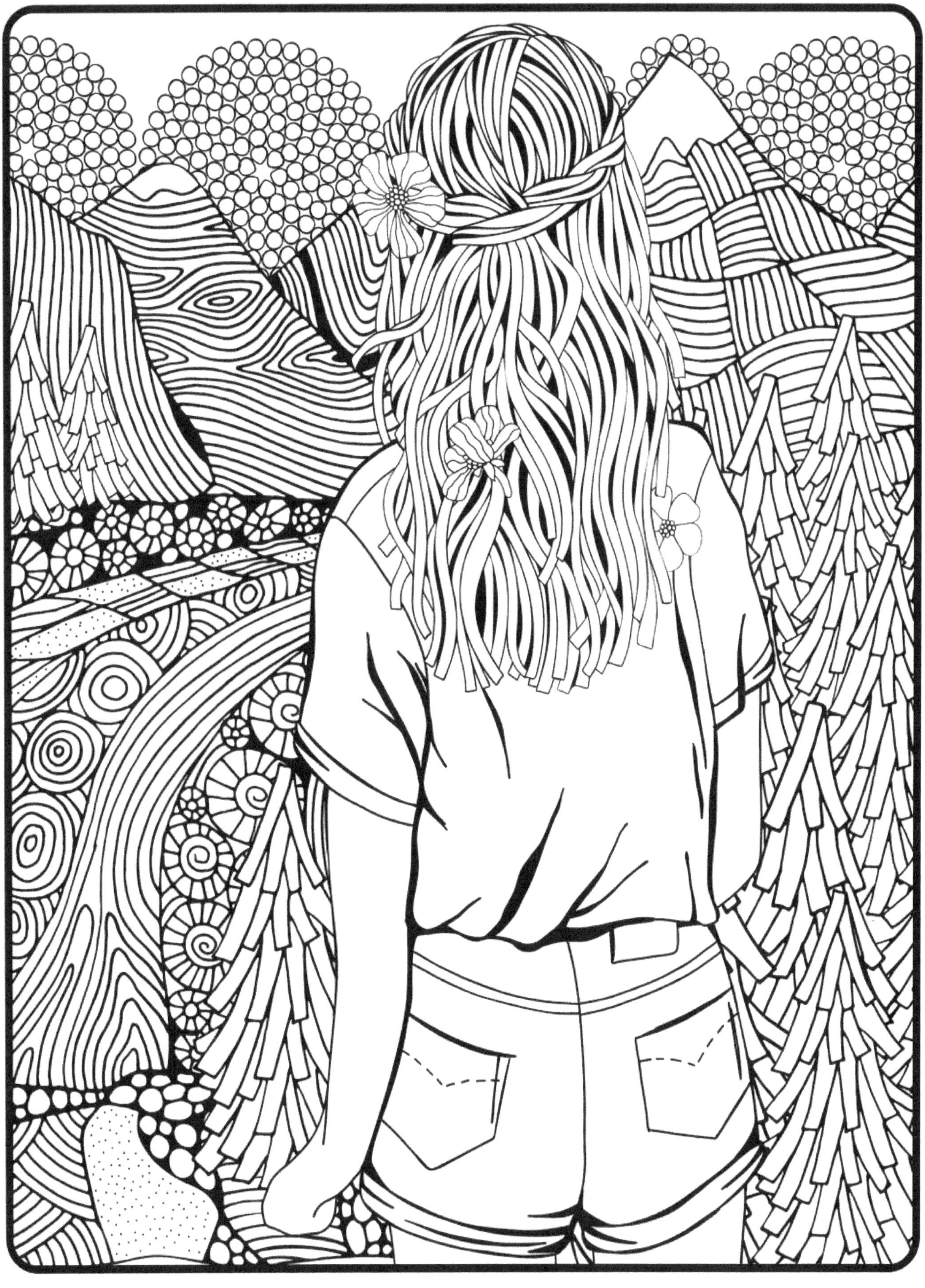

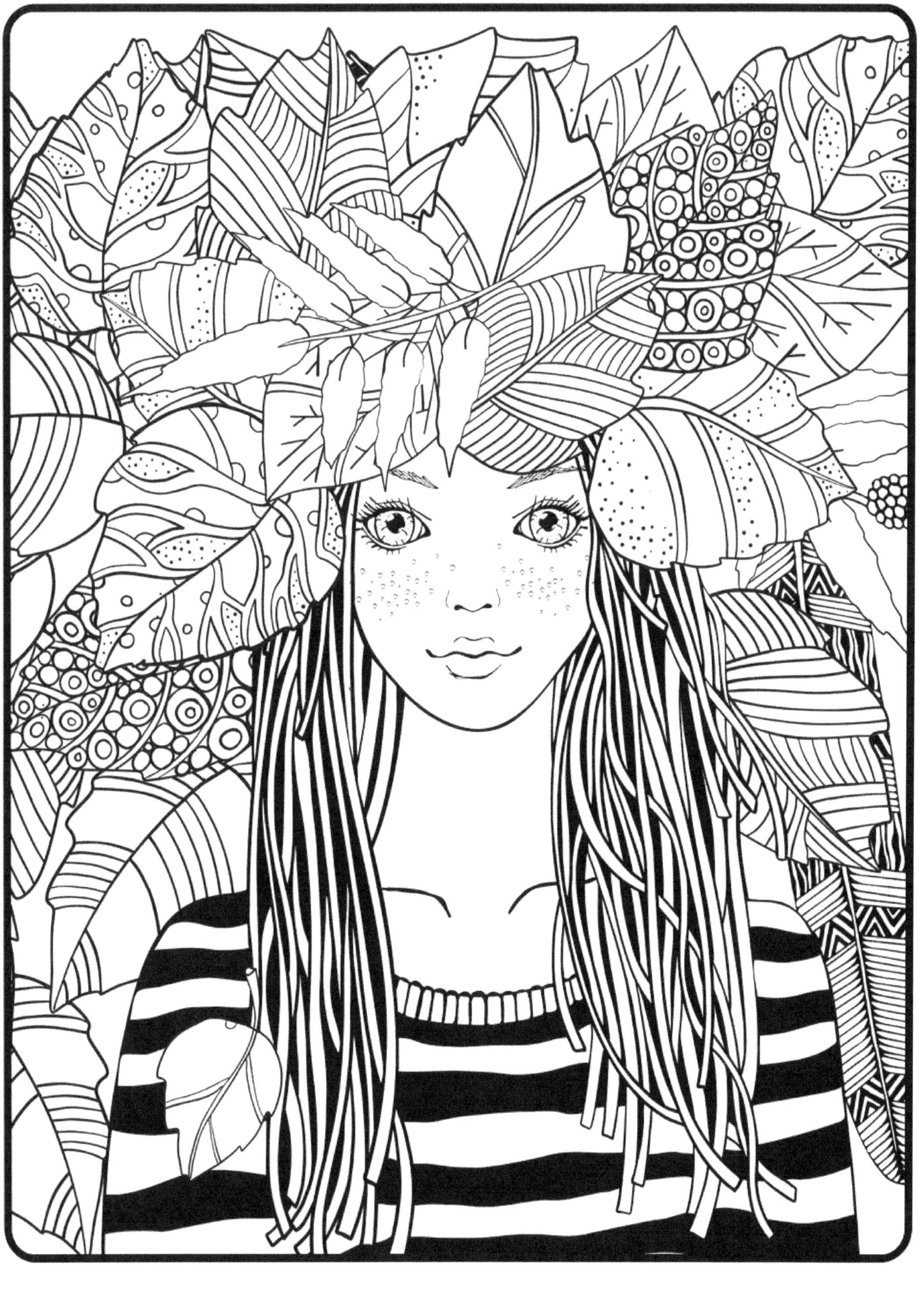

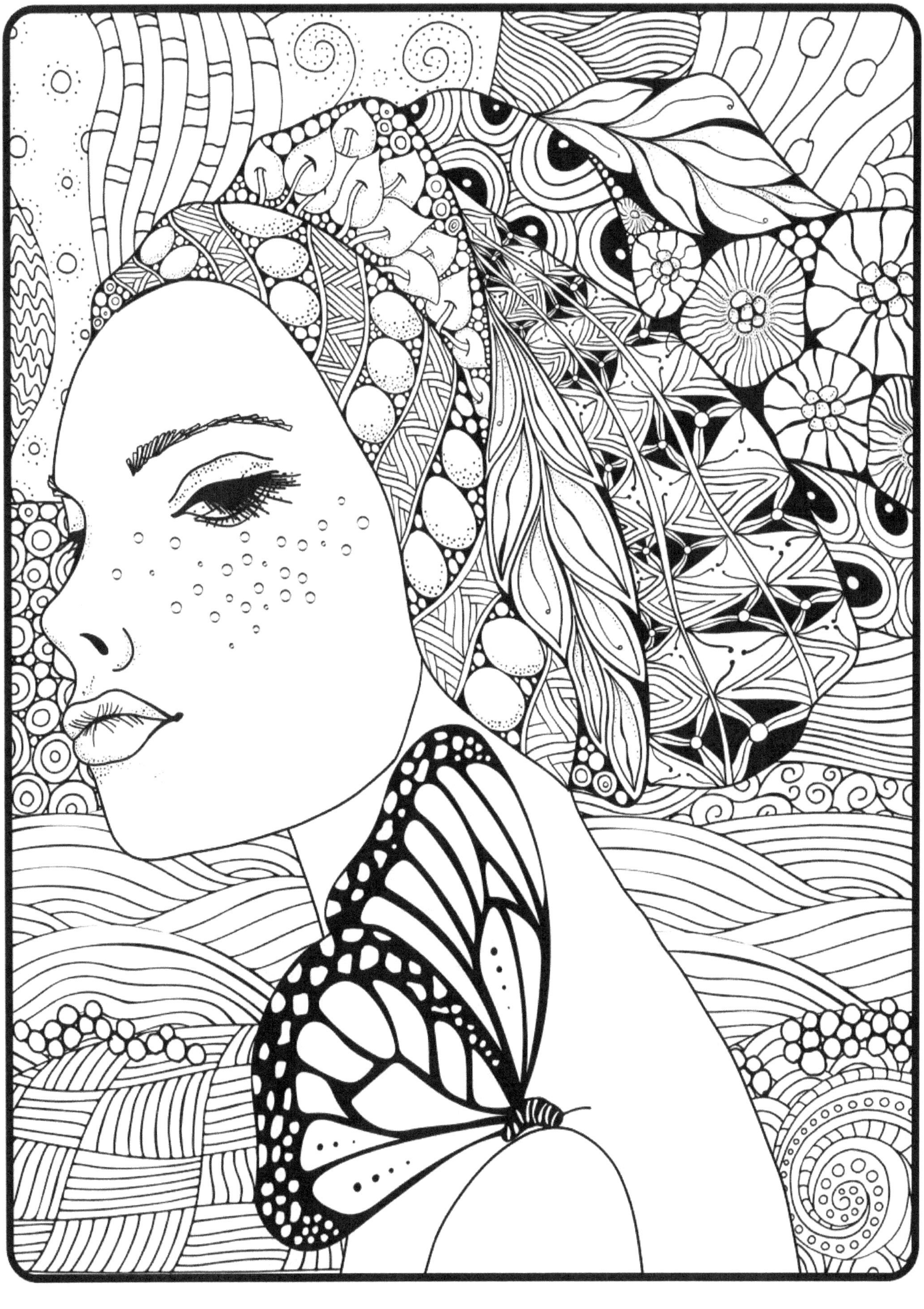

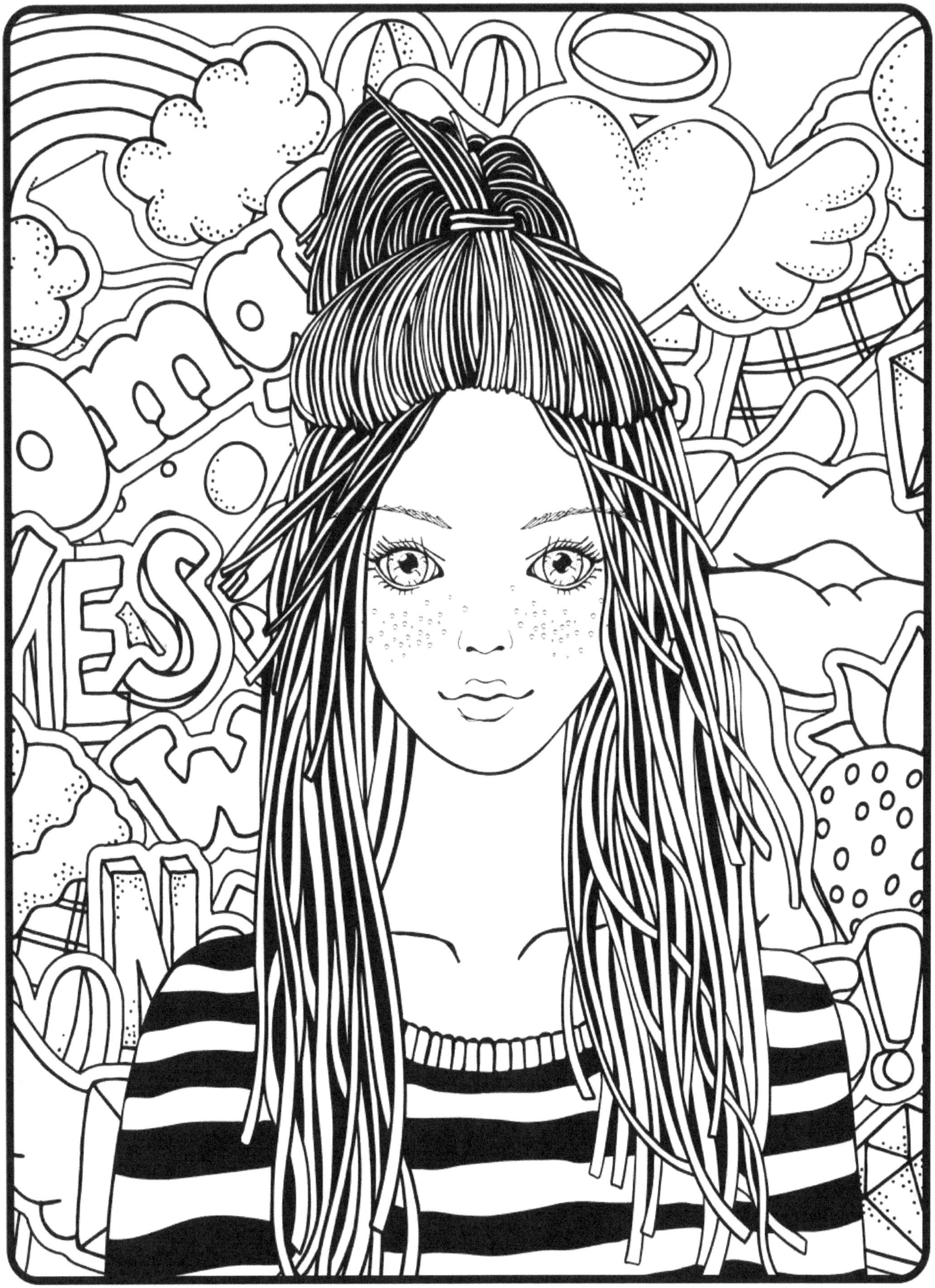
YES

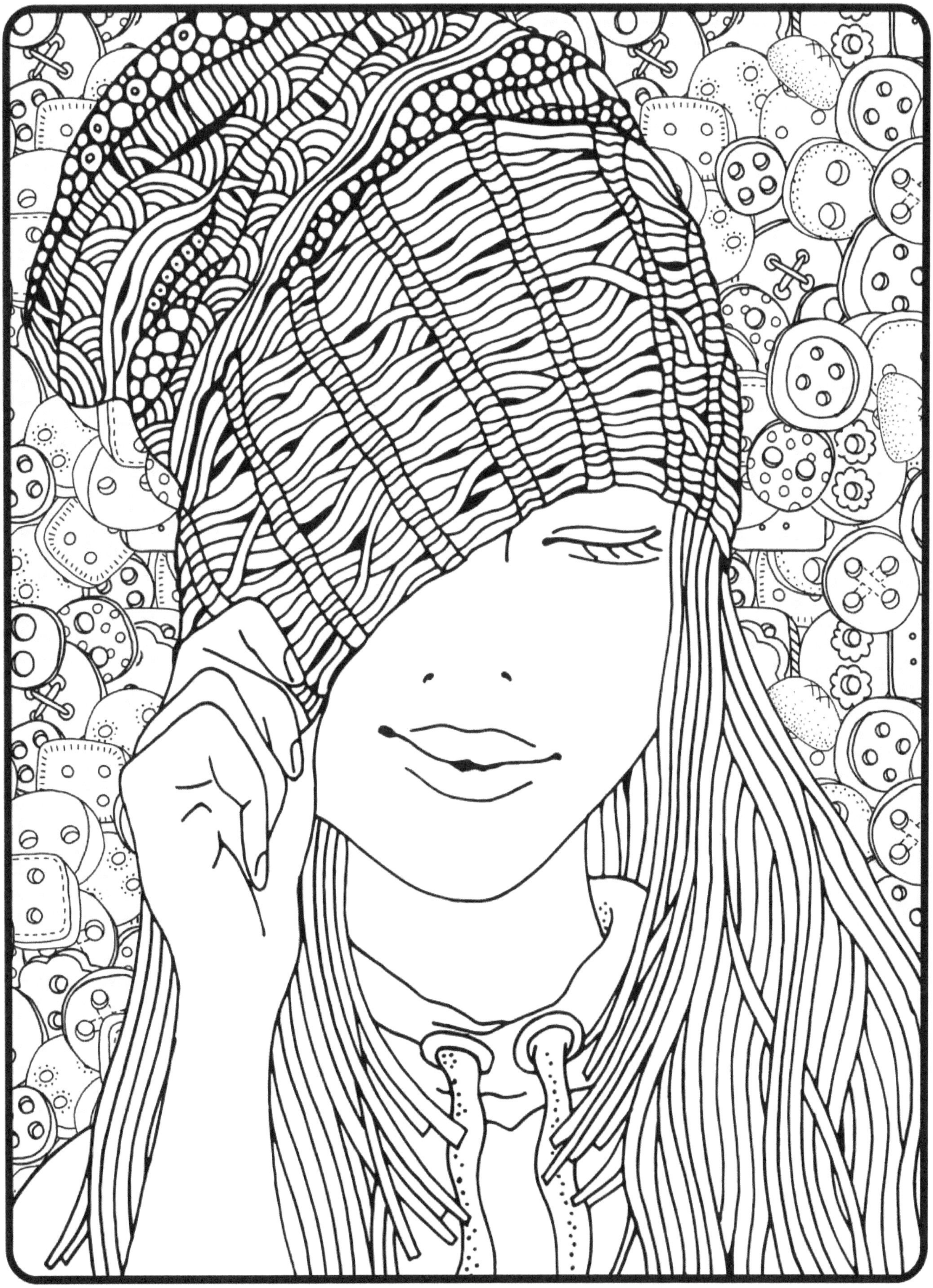

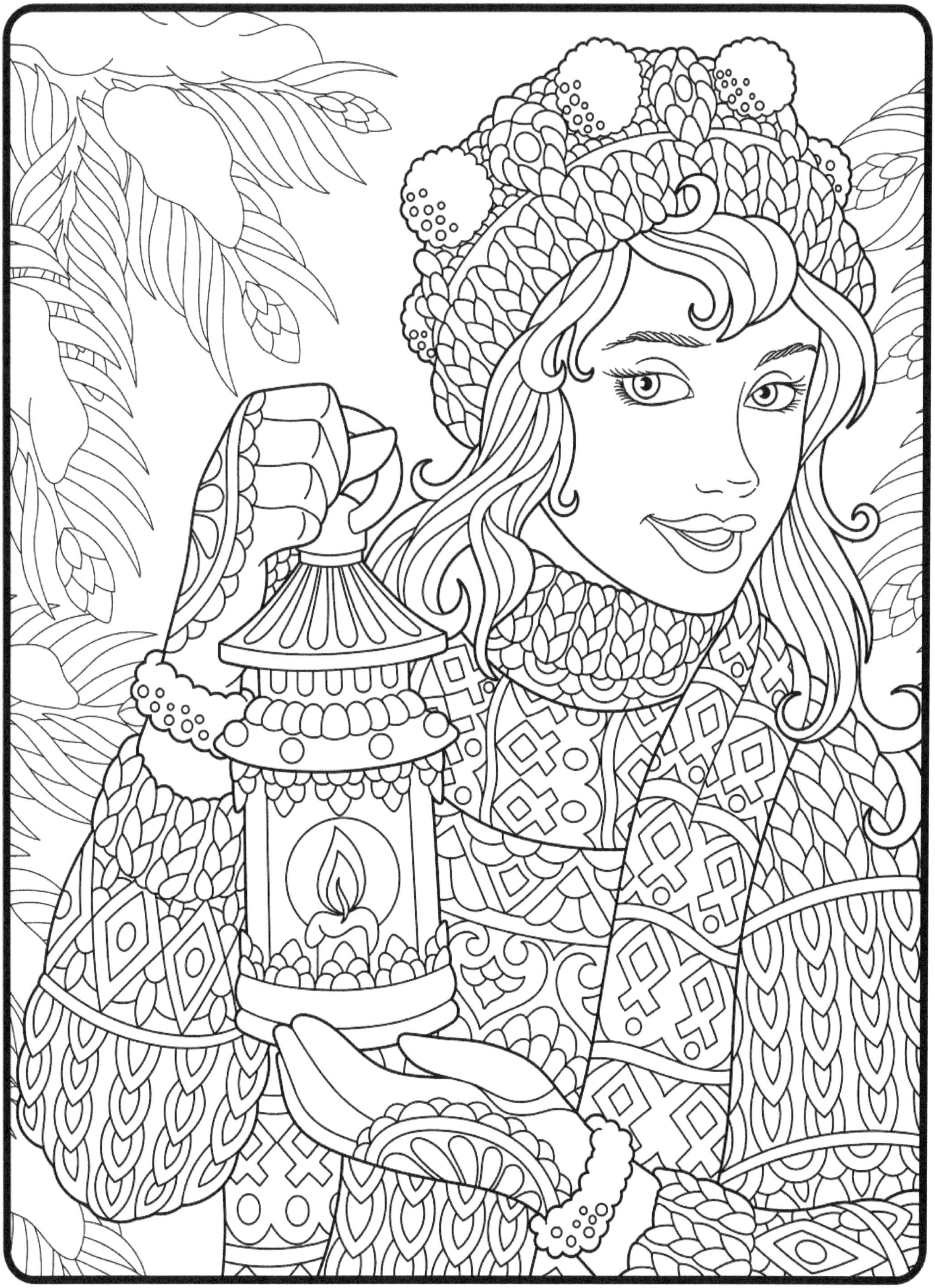

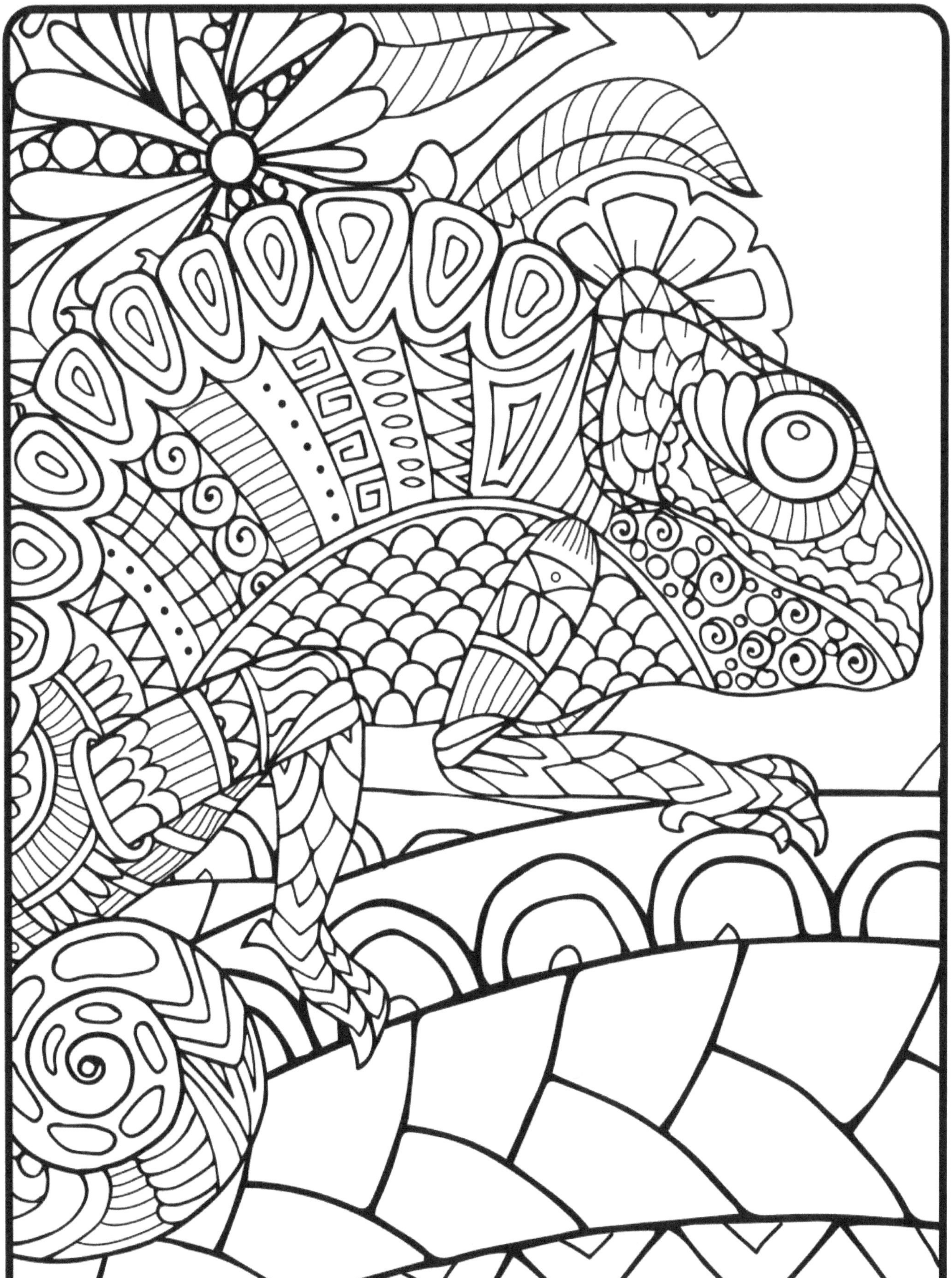

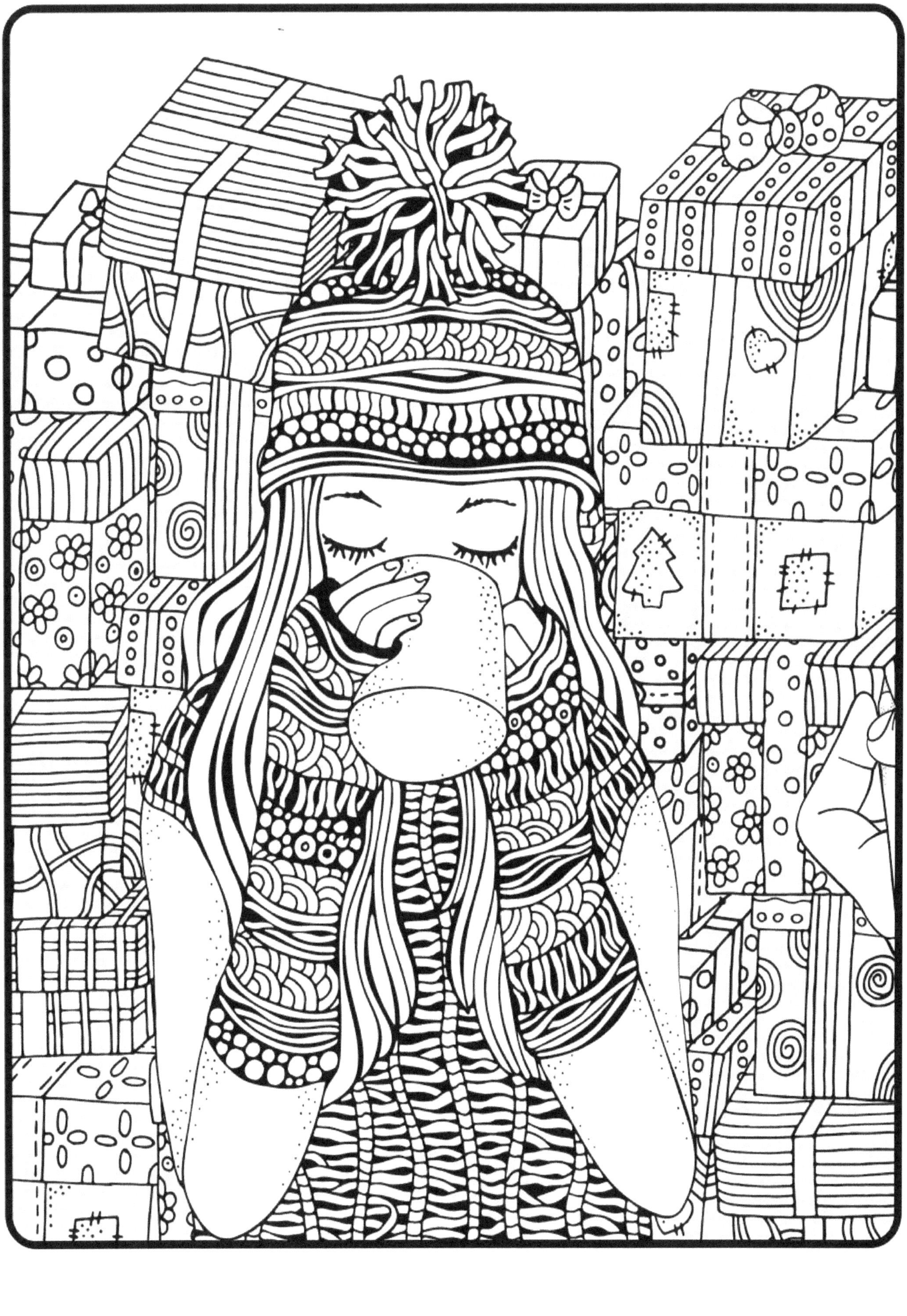

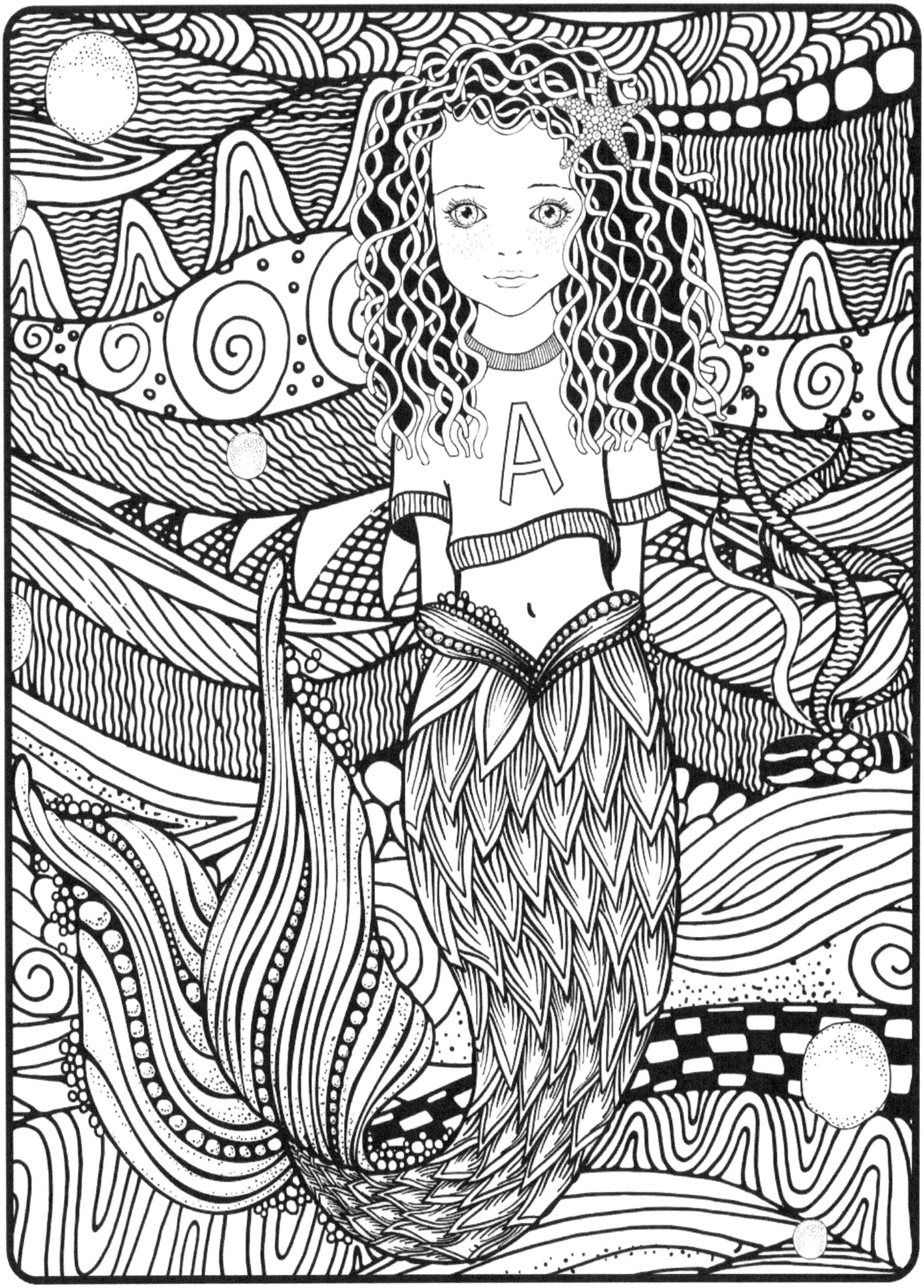
A

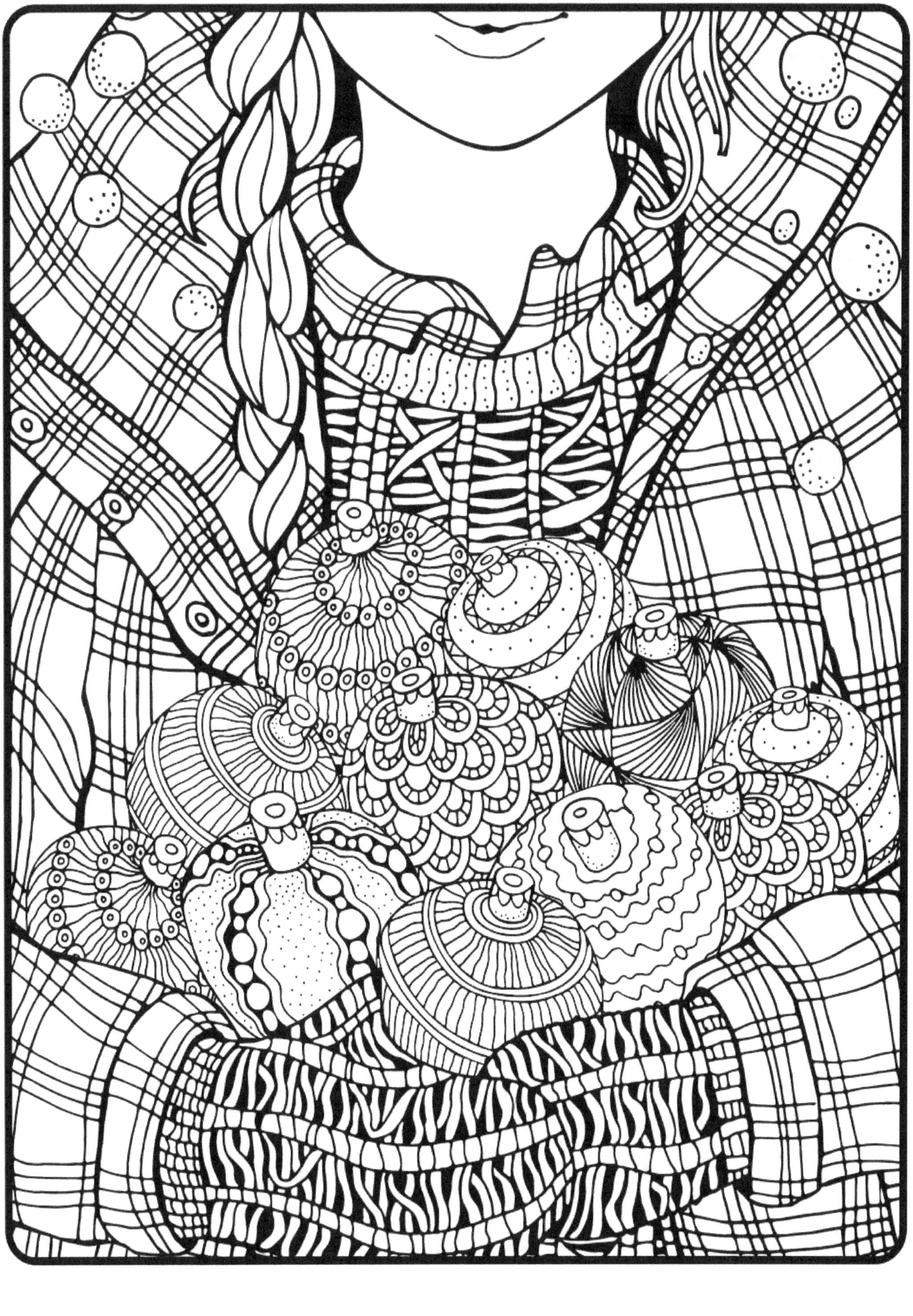

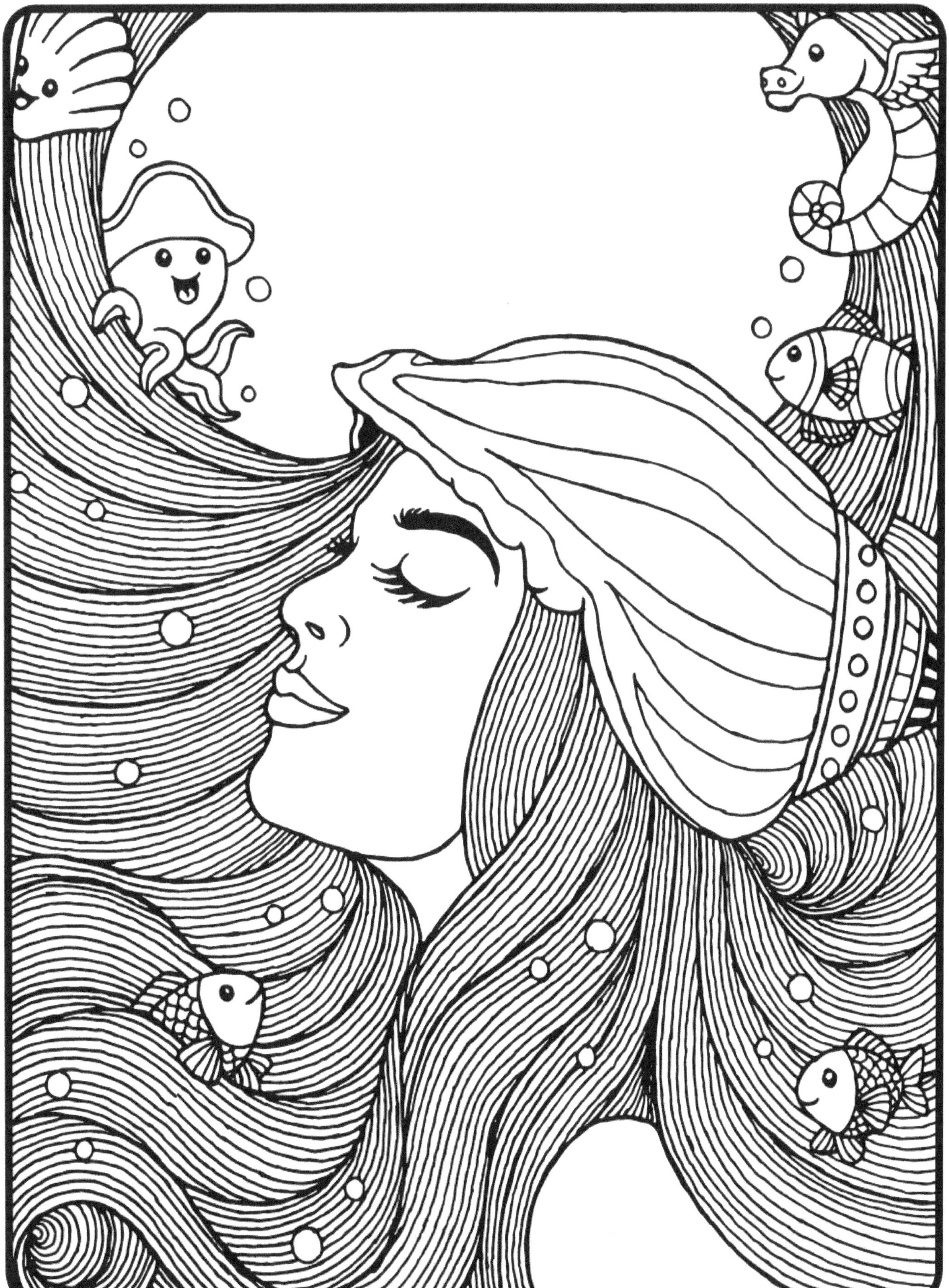

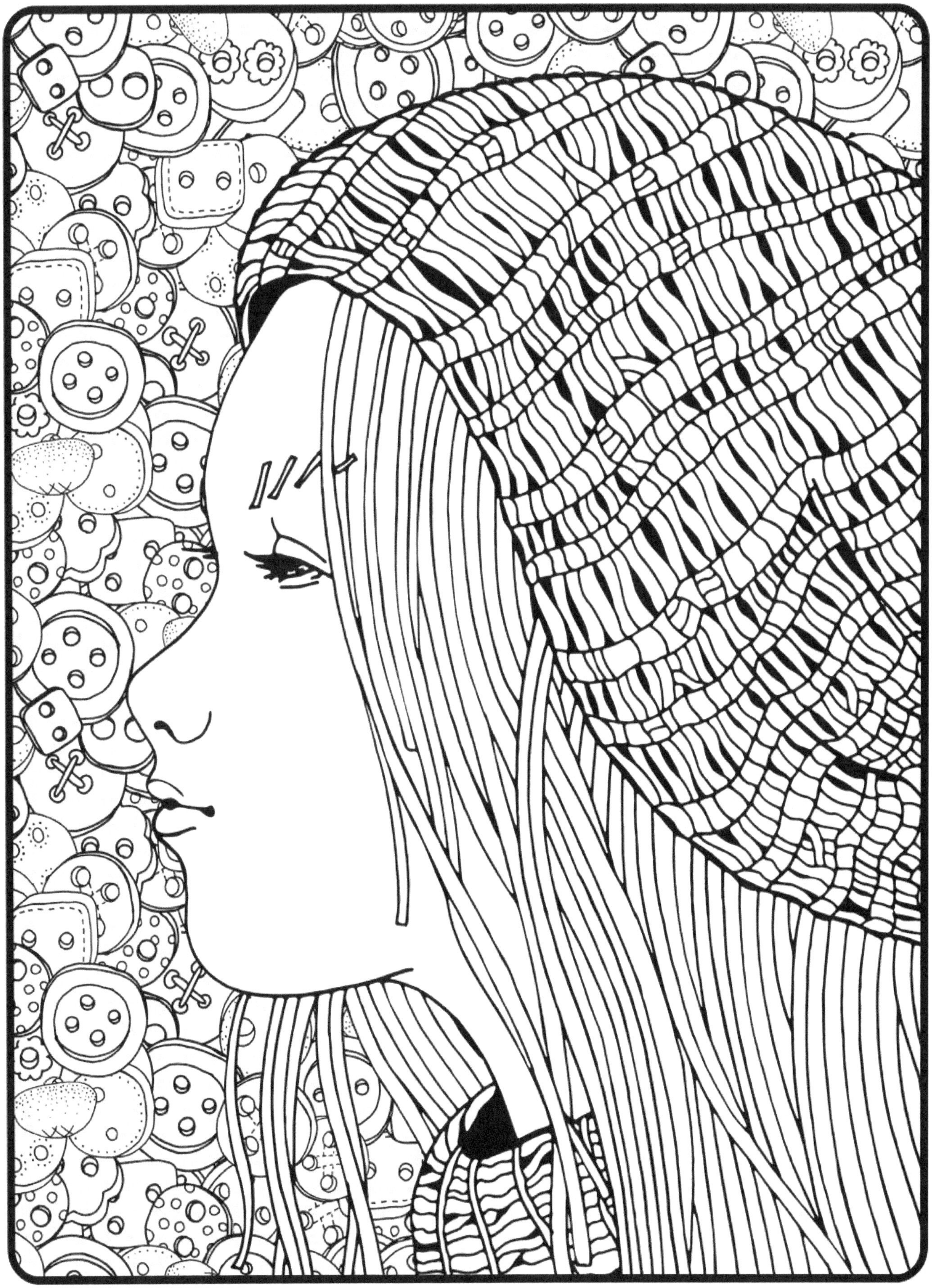

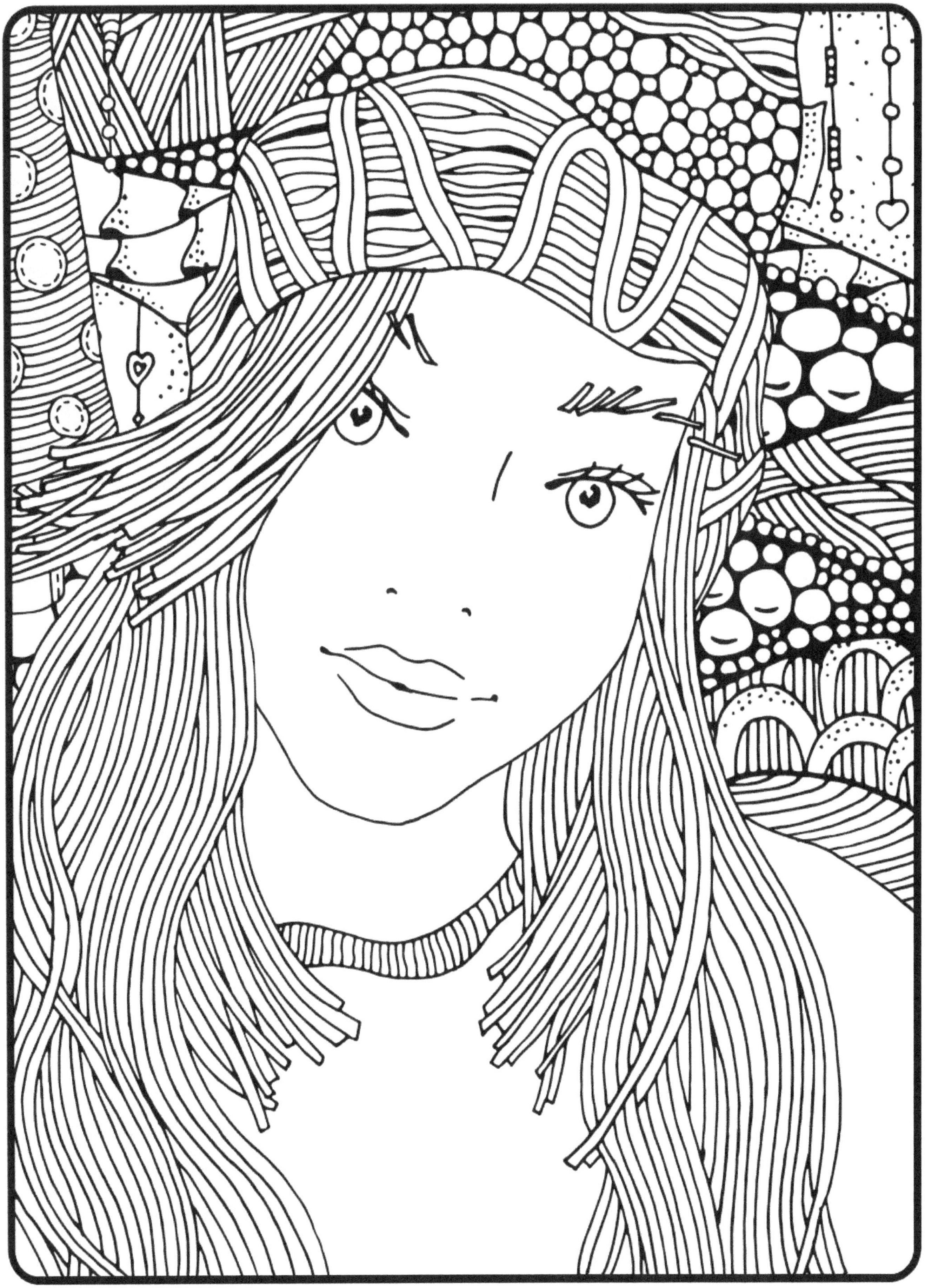

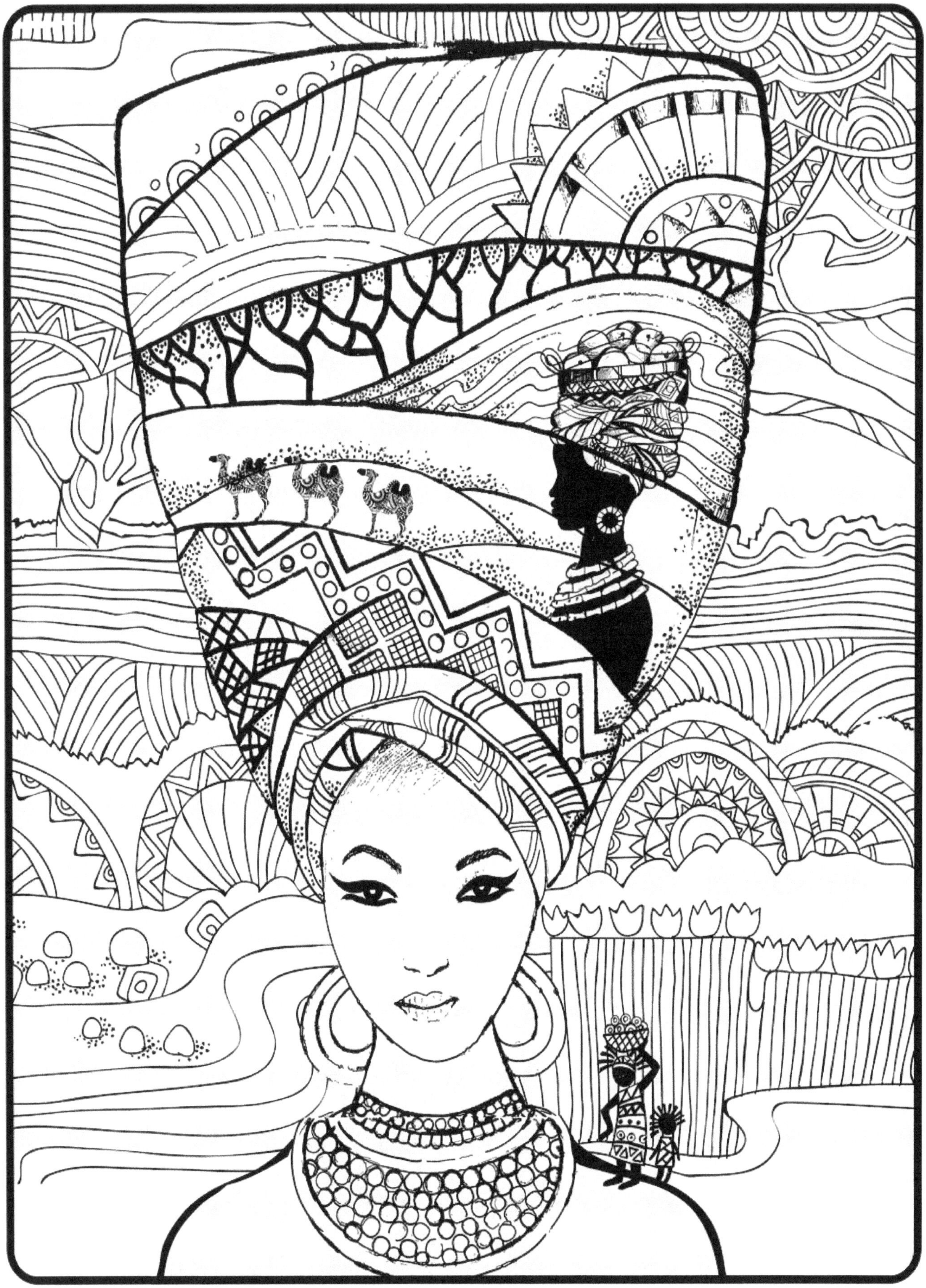

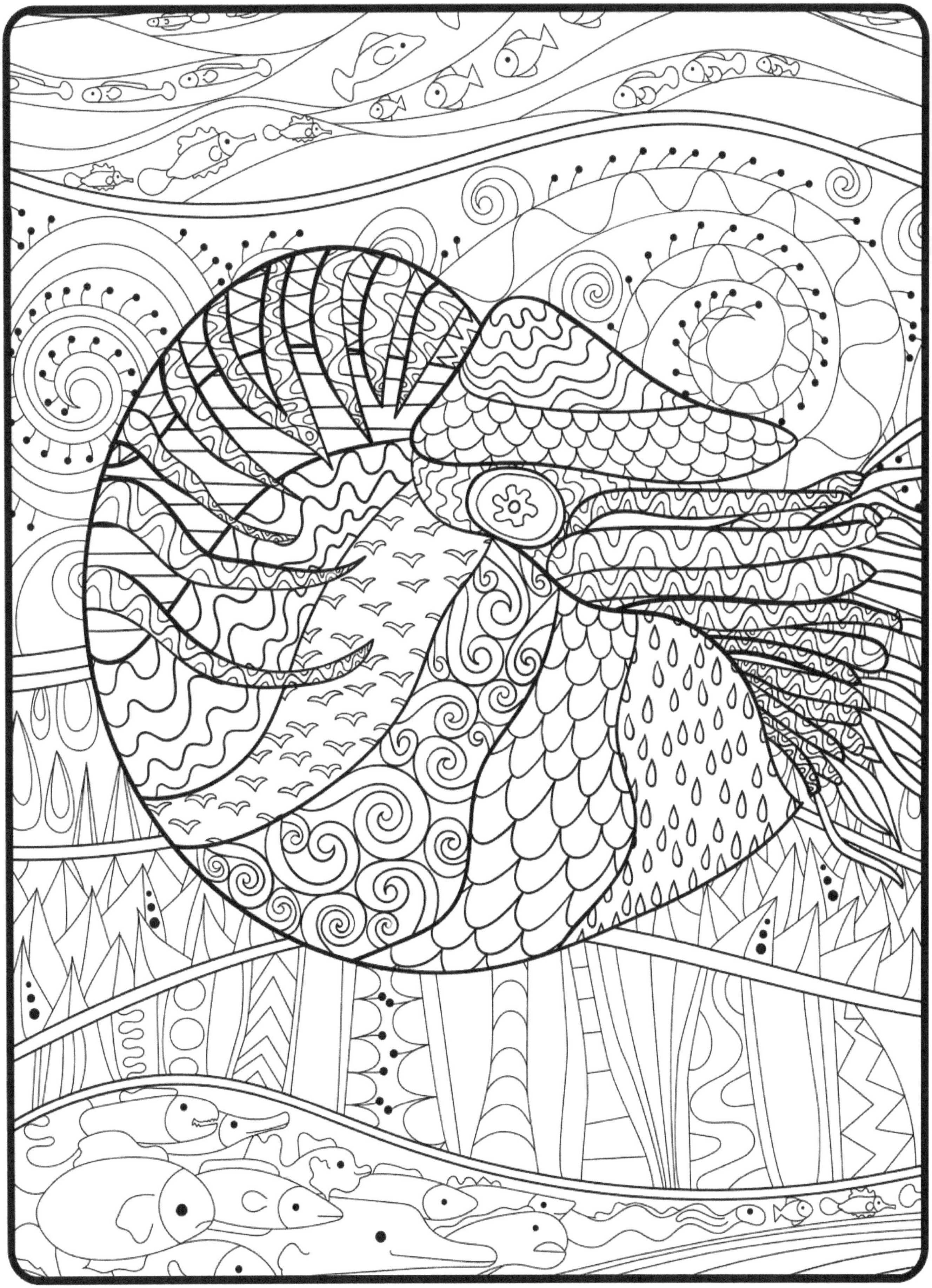

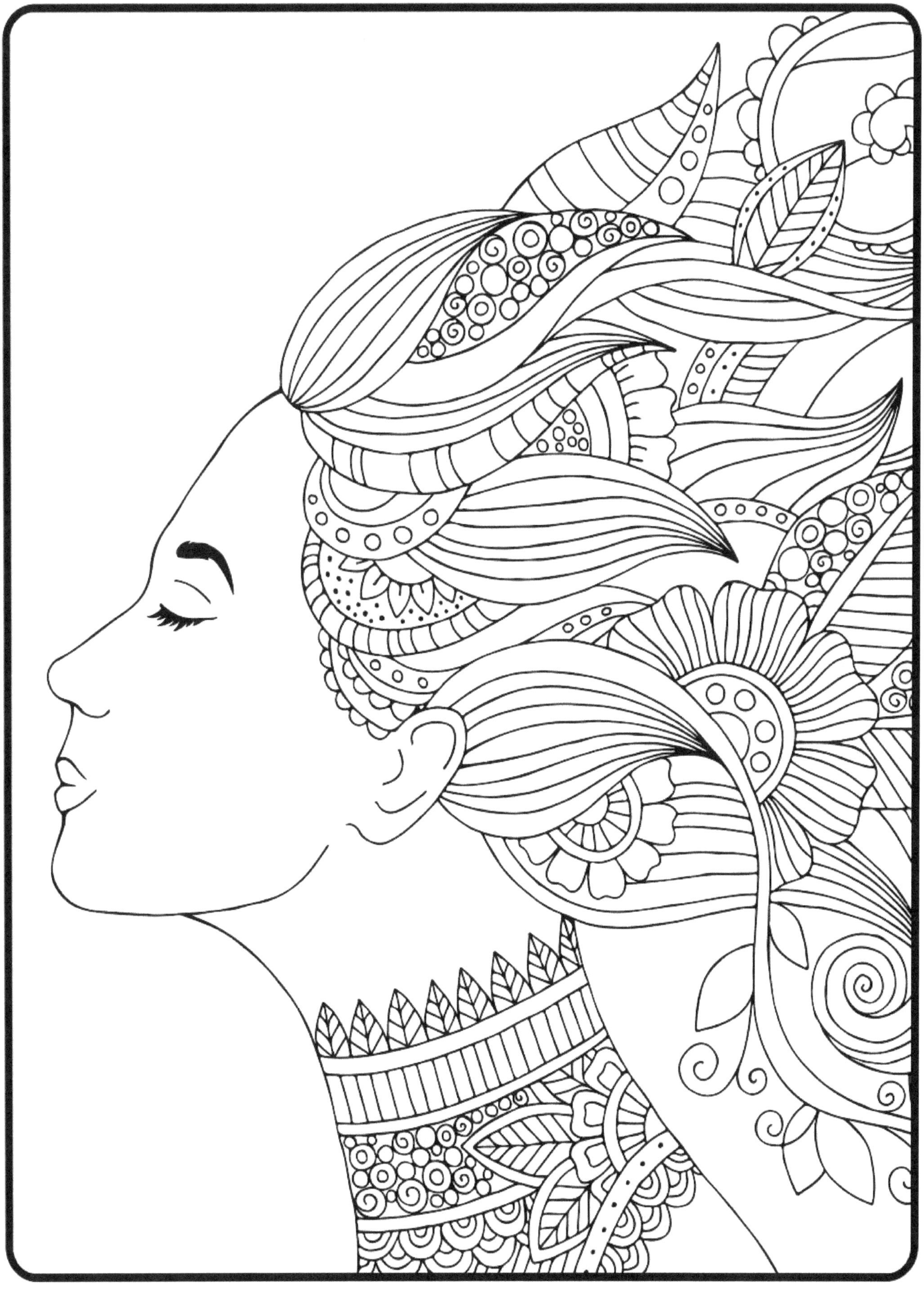

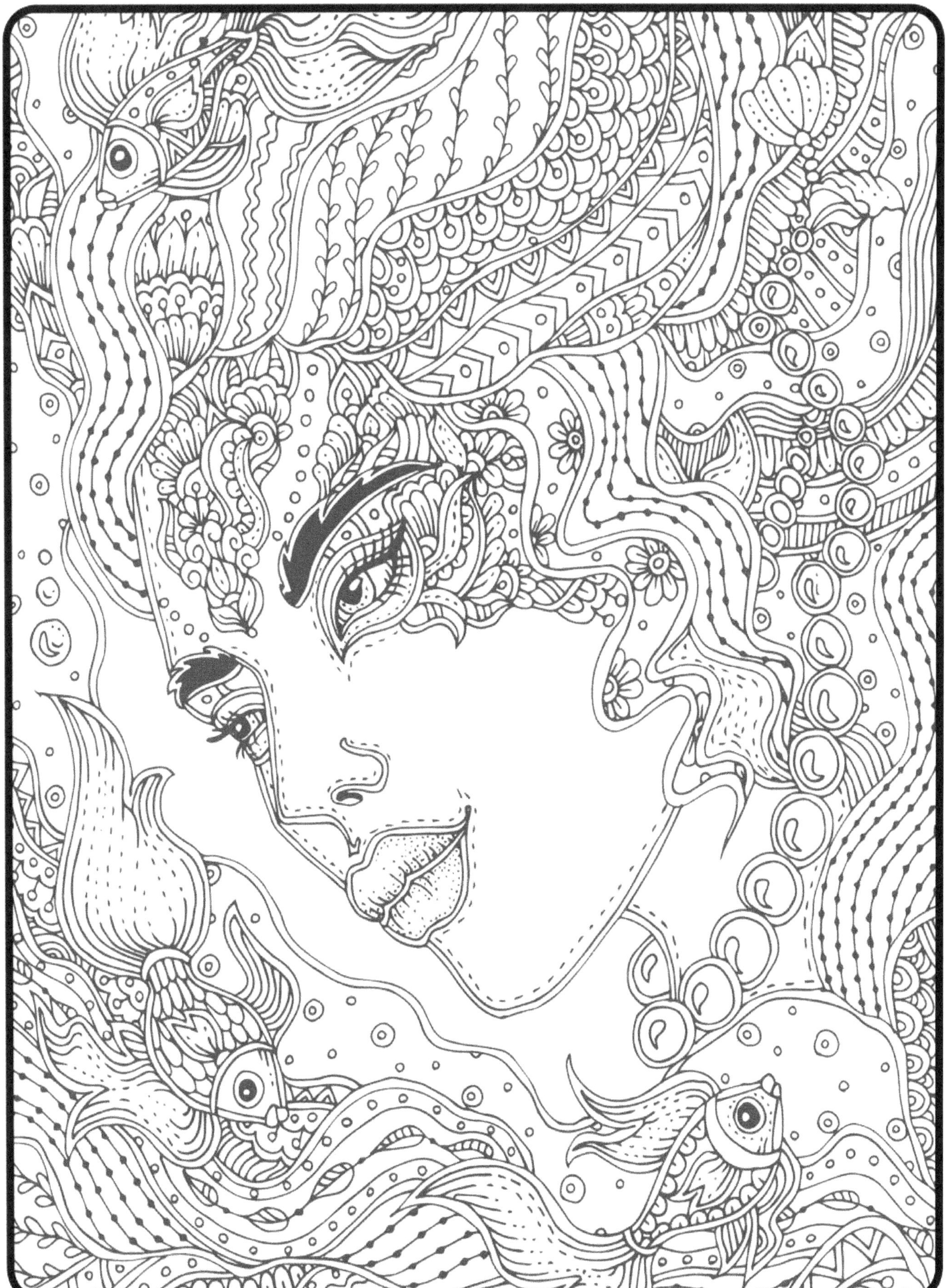

More coloring books from Katrin Stark

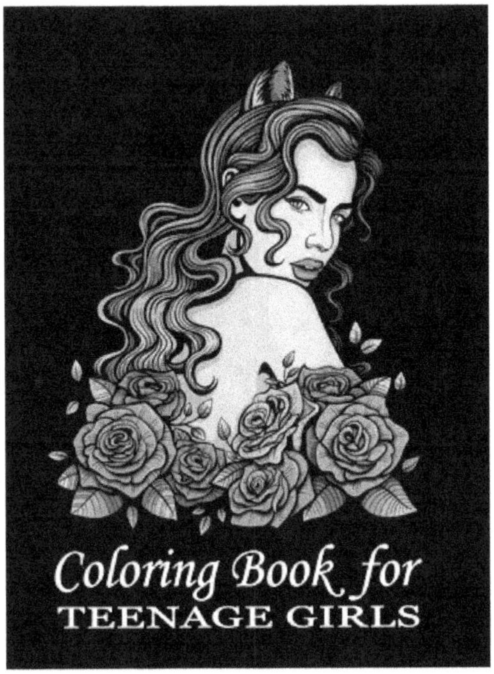

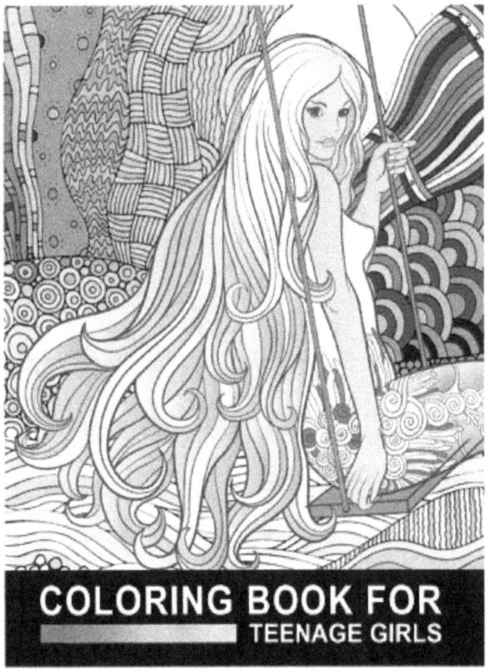

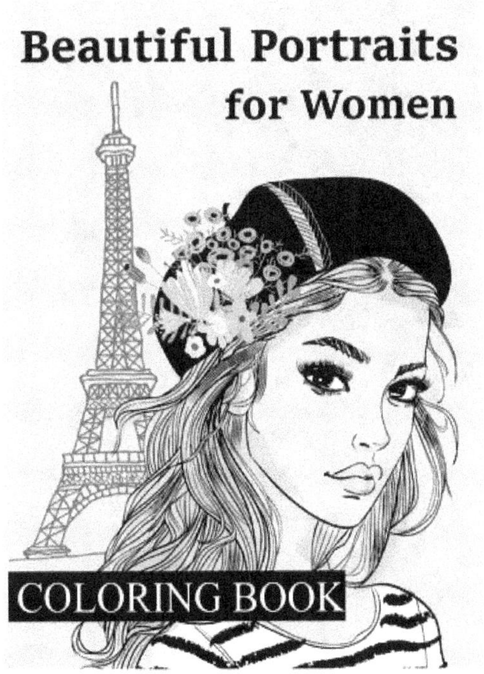

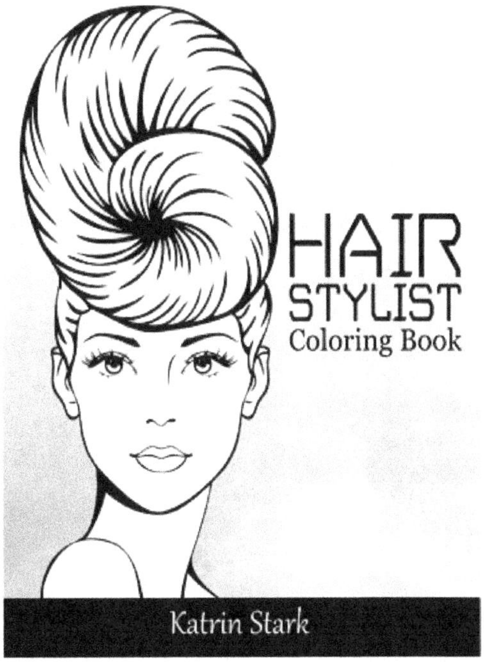

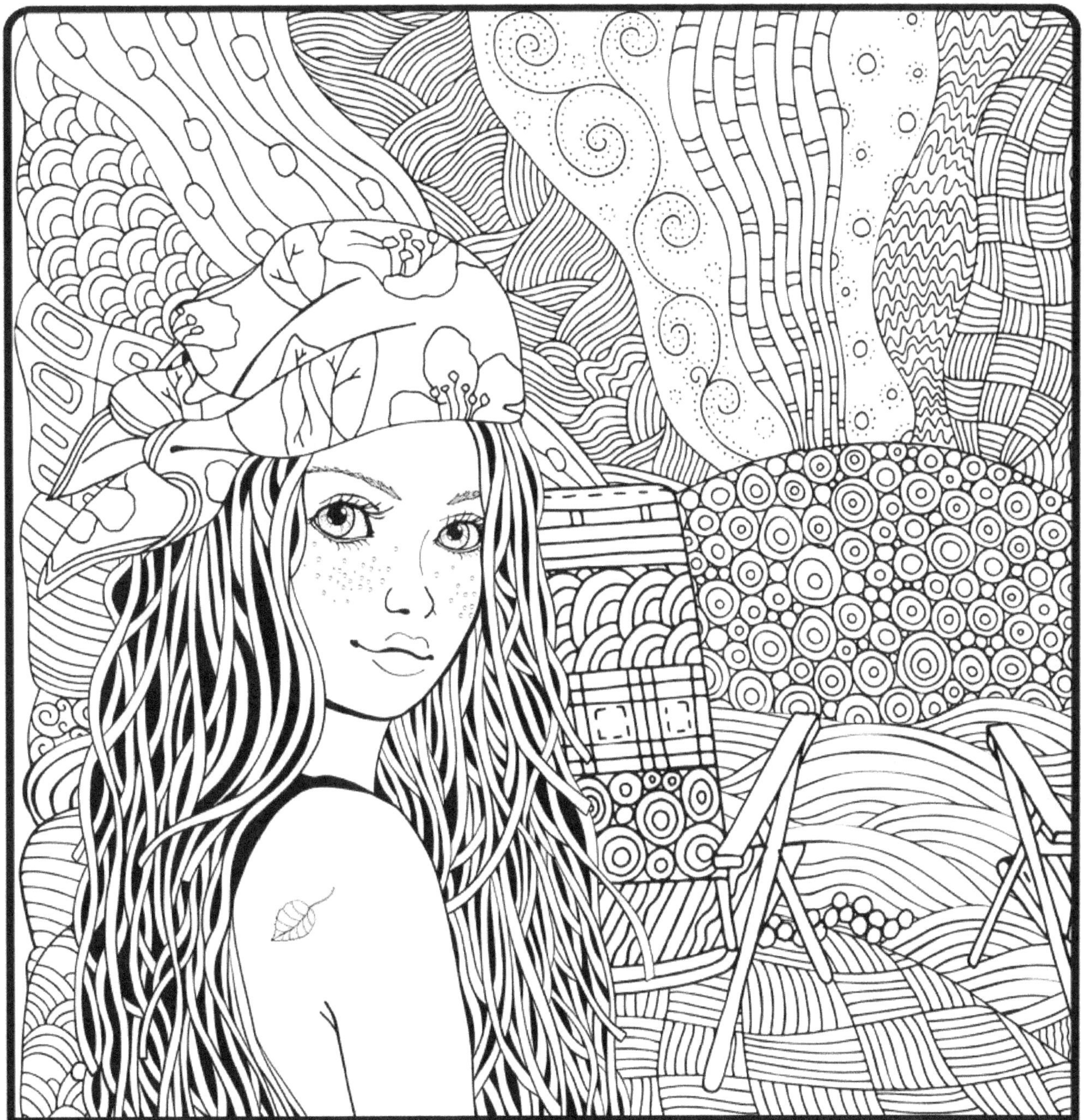

Thank you for buying this book

If you like the book, please consider leaving a review,

it will help author to create better books in the future

www.amazon.com/Katrin-Stark
www.amazon.co.uk/Katrin-Stark

www.ingramcontent.com/pod-product-compliance
Lightning Source LLC
Chambersburg PA
CBHW080519220526
45465CB00006B/2532
* 9 7 9 8 6 7 6 4 8 7 8 5 0 *